SALVATION

Lewis Sperry Chafer

Lewis Sperry Chafer, President of Dallas Theological Seminary, Dallas, Texas; Professor of Systematic Biblical Theology; Editor, Bibliotheca Sacra (C) Copyright, 1917, by LEWIS SPERRY CHAFER: In the Public domain

Published by Resurrected Books 2014

resurrectedbooks.com

This edition and printing,

FIRST EDITION

PRINTED IN U.S.A.

to my wife

MY DEAREST AND MOST FAITHFUL COMPANION
BOTH IN LIFE AND IN THE MINISTRY OF THE
WORD OF GOD, THIS BOOK IS AFFECTIONATELY
DEDICATED.

Table of Contents

PREFACE

This book is presented as a simple Gospel message and is in no way intended to be a contribution to theological discussion. It is evangelistic in purpose. The writer has hoped that this statement of God's saving grace may be adapted to the spiritual understanding of the unsaved that they may grasp the way of salvation from these pages and so be led to believe on the Lord Jesus Christ and be saved.

It is hoped, as well, that many who have believed may find some new consolation and upbuilding in Christ even through this brief unfolding of the saving grace of God.

That this book may be used of God to the eternal glory of His Son, Jesus Christ our Lord, is the prayer of the author.

Lewis Sperry Chafer.

October 1, 1917.

INTRODUCTION

When the young girl at Philippi described Paul and Silas as "servants of the Most High God which shew unto us the way of salvation," she unwittingly described them and their work in the truest and best possible way. There is nothing greater or nobler than to be "servants of the Most High God," and nothing more glorious than to "shew the way of salvation." This little work by my good friend, Mr. Chafer, is in the true "Apostolic Succession," for it depicts in clear and Scriptural language the Gospel of Divine salvation through the Person and Work of Christ. I rejoice in his faithful and forcible message, and am glad of the privilege of calling attention to a presentation of the way of salvation which is certain to lead all who read it earnestly to a living faith in Christ, and then to a constant joy because of the abundant and assured provision of God for the Christian life. It is only on the familiar principle of "Grace before Meat," so often associated with a clergyman, that I feel justified in accepting the invitation to commend these admirable chapters from one whose services as a Bible teacher are continually becoming better known and more warmly appreciated in the United States and Canada.

W. H. Griffith Thomas.

CHAPTER I

THE WORD SALVATION

The word salvation is used in the Bible to indicate a work of God in behalf of man. In the present dispensation its use is limited to His work for individuals only, and is vouchsafed to them upon one definite condition. Too much emphasis cannot be placed on the fact that now, according to the Bible, salvation is the result of the work of God for the individual, rather than the work of the individual for God, or even the work of the individual for himself. Eventually the one who is saved by the power of God may, after that divine work is accomplished, do "good works" for God; for salvation is said to be "unto good works" (Eph. 2:10) and those who "believed" are to be "careful to maintain good works" (Tit. 3:8). Good works are evidently made possible by salvation; but these good works, which follow salvation, do not add anything to the all-sufficient and perfect saving work of God.

As used in the New Testament, the word salvation may indicate all or a part of the divine undertaking. When the reference is to all of the work of God, the whole transformation is in view from the estate wherein one is lost and condemned to the final appearance of that one in the image of Christ in glory. This larger use of the word, therefore, combines in it many separate works of God for the individual, such as Atonement, Grace, Propitiation, Forgiveness, Justification, Imputation, Regeneration, Adoption, Sanctification, Redemption and Glorification. The two following passages describe the estate from which and the estate into which the individual is saved: "Wherefore remember, that ye being in times past Gentiles in the flesh, who are called Uncircumcision by that which is called the Circumcision in the flesh made by hands; that at that time ye were without Christ, being aliens from the commonwealth of Israel, and strangers from the covenants of promise, having no hope, and without God in the world" (Eph. 2:11, 12). "Behold, what manner of love the Father hath bestowed upon us, that we should be called the sons of God: therefore the world knoweth us not, because it knew Him not. Beloved, now are we the sons of God, and it doth not yet appear what we shall be: but we know that, when he shall appear, we shall be like him; for we shall see him as he is" (1 John 3:1-2). There could be no greater contrast of possible estates for man than those described in these passages.

This transformation, it must be conceded, rather than representing the greatest thing impotent man can do for God, represents the greatest thing the infinite God can do for man; for there is nothing to be conceived of beyond the estate to which this salvation brings one, namely, "like Christ" and "conformed to the image of his Son."

Much of the whole divine undertaking in salvation is accomplished in the saved one at the moment he exercises saving faith. So, also, some portions of this work are in the form of a process of transformation after the first work is wholly accomplished. And again, there is a phase of the divine undertaking which is revealed as consummating the whole work of God at the moment of its completion. This last aspect of salvation is wholly future.

Salvation, then, in the present dispensation, may be considered in three tenses as it is revealed in the Scriptures: the past, or that part of the work which already is wholly accomplished in and for the one who has believed; the present, or that which is now being accomplished in and for the one who has believed; and the future, or that which will be accomplished to complete the work of God in and for the one who has believed.

The following passages are clear statements of these various aspects of the one divine undertaking:

I. The child of God was saved from the guilt and penalty of sin when he believed: "And he said to the woman, Thy faith hath saved thee; go in peace" (Lk. 7:50); "And brought them out, and said, Sirs, what must I do to be saved? And they said, Believe on the Lord Jesus Christ and thou shalt be saved and thy house" (Acts 16:30, 31); "For the preaching of the cross is to them that perish foolishness; but unto us which are saved it is the power of God" (1 Cor. 1:18); "For we are unto God a sweet savor of Christ, in them that are saved, and in them that perish" (2 Cor. 2:15); "For by grace are ye saved through faith; and that not of yourselves: it is the gift of God" (Eph. 2:8); "Who hath saved us, and called us with an holy calling, not according to our works, but according to his own purpose and grace, which was given us in Christ Jesus before the world began" (2 Tim. 1:9).

II. The child of God, constituted such through belief, is being saved from the power and domination of sin on the same principle of faith: "Sanctify them through thy truth: thy word is truth" (John 17:17); "For sin shall not have dominion over you: for ye are not under the law, but under grace" (Rom. 6:14); "Wherefore, my beloved, as ye have always obeyed, not as in my presence only, but now much more in my absence, work out your own salvation with fear and trembling. For it is God which worketh in you both to will and to do of his good pleasure" (Phil. 2:12, 13); "For the law of the Spirit of life in Christ Jesus hath made me free from the law of sin and death" (Rom. 8:2); "This I say then, Walk in the Spirit, and ye shall not fulfill the lust of the flesh" (Gal. 5:16).

III. The child of God, begotten as such through belief, is yet to be saved from the presence of sin into the presence of God: "And that, knowing the time, that now it is high time to awake out of sleep: for now is our salvation nearer than when we believed" (Rom. 13:11); "Blessed be the God and Father of our Lord Jesus Christ, which according to his abundant mercy hath begotten us again unto a lively hope by the resurrection of Jesus Christ from the dead. To an inheritance incorruptible, and undefiled, and that fadeth not away, reserved in heaven for you, who are kept by the power of God through faith unto salvation ready to be revealed in the last time" (1 Pet. 1:3-5); "Behold, what manner of love the Father hath bestowed upon us, that we should be called the sons of God: therefore the world knoweth us not, because it knew him not. Beloved now are we the sons of God, and it doth not yet appear what we shall be: but we know that, when he shall appear, we shall be like him; for we shall see him as he is" (1 John 3:1-2).

So, again, there are passages in which these various time aspects in salvation are all combined: "Being confident of this very thing, that he which hath begun a good work in you will perform it until the day of Jesus Christ" (Phil. 1:6); "But of him are ye in Christ Jesus, who of God is made unto us wisdom, and righteousness, and sanctification, and redemption" (1 Cor. 1:30); "Even as Christ also loved the church, and gave himself for it; that he might sanctify and cleanse it with the washing of water by the word. That he might present it to himself a glorious church, not having spot, or wrinkle, or any such thing; but that it should be holy and without blemish" (Eph. 5:25-27)4

CHAPTER II

GOD'S ESTIMATE OF THE LOST

At no point is faith more tested than in receiving the divine estimate of the present estate and destiny of all who are not saved; yet the record stands on the sacred page and is as much a part of God's revelation of truth as is the more winsome disclosure concerning the saved and heaven. In vain does man struggle to deliver himself from the dread and shadow of the former while still attempting to retain the comfort and light of the latter. Even a blinded, unregenerate mind must be convinced of the unreasonableness of selecting only desirable elements out of the unitive whole of divine revelation. If man can dispose of the dark picture which describes the estate of the lost, he has, by that process, surrendered all claim to authority and all ground of assurance in those Scriptures which describe the estate of the saved.

Man is prone to disregard the plain boundary lines of distinction between the saved and the unsaved as indicated in the Bible. He is naturally occupied with the temporal things that are seen, and is by nature blind to the eternal things (1 Cor. 2:14; 2 Cor. 4:3, 4; John 3:3) which are not seen. He is inclined to conceive of salvation as resulting from a manner of daily life, both moral and religious, rather than a state wrought by the creative power of God. An appeal for a reformed manner of life is to him "practical" and "reasonable," and he sees little value in the Biblical appeal for personal faith in the saving power and grace of God. A saved person, by his new life from God, may live on a higher plane, and certainly will; but to attempt to live on a higher plain will not, and cannot, impart the new life, or save a lost soul. The unsaved, according to the Bible, include all who have not been accepted by God through a personal trust in the crucified and risen Saviour. All moral and religious people are not, therefore, according to the divine conditions, to be counted among the saved. Paul prayed for Israel "that they might be saved" (Rom. 10:1, 2), and those for whom he prayed, it should be remembered, were the very ones of whom he wrote in this same passage that they had "a zeal for God" and went about "to establish their own righteousness." We know, also, that they fasted, and prayed, and gave a tithe of all they possessed; yet, in spite of all this, the faithful, inspired Apostle prays that they might be saved. To be saved was evidently, in the Apostle's mind, more than the diligent effort along the lines of moral and religious practices.

The Bible sharply distinguishes between the saved and the unsaved, and in its classification, of necessity, wholly ignores what may seem reasonable or unreasonable in the sphere of human life. It bases its distinctions on the eternal necessities and provisions within the larger sphere of the kingdom of God. Here the important issues of conduct and service are not first to be considered. The deeper reality of an entire new nature is rather the primary objective, and no good works can take its place. It is as terrible for a church member, or minister, to be lost as for any one else. Certainly there is nothing in the fact of church membership, ordinances, or the preaching profession that can take the place of the Biblical requirement for salvation, or mitigate the final doom that is assured to those who reject the Saviour. The five virgins who possessed every outward appearance and profession were, nevertheless, without the oil which is the symbol of the divine life. In spite of all their religious externals they heard it said, "I know you not." "Not every one that saith unto me, Lord, Lord, shall enter into the kingdom of heaven; but he that doeth the will of my Father which is in heaven. Many will say to me in that day, Lord, Lord, have we not prophesied in thy name? and in thy name have cast out devils? and in thy name done many wonderful works? And then will I profess unto them, I never knew you: depart from me, ye that work iniquity" (Mt. 7:21-23). "Jesus answered and said unto them, This is the work of God, that ye believe on him whom he hath sent" (John 6:29).

The estate of the unsaved is described in the Bible by positive terms: "For the Son of man is come to seek and to save that which was lost" (Lk. 19:10); "For God so loved the world, that he gave his only begotten Son, that whosoever believeth in him should not perish, but have everlasting life"; "He that believeth on him is not condemned: but he that believeth not is condemned already, because he hath not believed in the name of the only begotten Son of God. And this is the condemnation that light is come into the world, and men loved darkness rather than light, because their deeds were evil. For every one that doeth evil hateth the light, neither cometh to the light, lest his deeds should be reproved" (John 3:16, 18-20). "He that believeth on the Son hath everlasting life: and he that believeth not the Son shall not see life; but the wrath of God abideth on him" (John 3:36). "Ye are of your father the devil, and the lusts of your father ye will do. He was a murderer from the beginning, and abode not in the truth, because there is no truth in him. When he speaketh a lie, he speaketh of his own: for he is a liar, and the father of it" (John 8:44); "Wherein in time past ye walked according to the course of this world, according to the prince of the power of the air, the spirit that now worketh in the children of disobedience" (Eph. 2:2); "For from within, out of the heart of men, proceed evil thoughts, adulteries, fornications, murders, thefts, covetousness, wickedness, deceit, lasciviousness, an evil eye, blasphemy, pride, foolishness: all these evil things come from within, and defile the man" (Mk. 7:21-23).

In Eph. 2:1-2 the contrast between the saved and the unsaved is first drawn at the point of possessing or not possessing the divine life: "And you hath he quickened, who were dead in trespasses and sins; wherein in time past ye walked according to the course of this world, according to the prince of the power of the air, the spirit that now worketh in the children of disobedience." This death is not physical, for the dead ones are said to be "walking according to the course of this world," the aspirations of which walk are centered in the things of the world system. They are also said to be "walking according to the prince of the power of the air (Satan), the spirit that now worketh in (energizeth) the children of disobedience." This classification, "the children of disobedience," includes all who have not been "made alive" by the power of God. Disobedience here is a state of being and is federal rather than personal. "By one man's disobedience (Adam) many were made sinners." So, also, "by the obedience of one (Christ) shall many be made righteous." Thus the acceptableness of the saved one is also a state and is federal rather than personal. He being in Christ is a child of obedience; the unsaved one being in

Adam is a child of disobedience. In Adam disobedient and lost; in Christ obedient, righteous and acceptable to God (Rom. 5:19; Eph. 1:6). "He became obedient unto death, even the death of the cross." Before the infinite holiness of God no person, saved or unsaved, can rightfully claim, within his own merit, to be obedient and righteous in the sight of God; yet the weakest person who stands in Christ is, by virtue of that position, a child of obedience in the sight of God.

In all the children of disobedience, regardless of professions or conduct, Satan is here said to be the energizing power. The energy of this mighty being may inspire refinement, education, culture, and the externals of religion, for it is not against these external virtues that Satan is opposed. His enmity is intelligently directed against the saving grace of God, which is a widely differing issue from that which the problems of personal conduct present.

Satan is said to be energizing the unsaved within all the spheres of their present activity. In like manner, the saved are said to be energized by God: "For it is God which worketh in you both to will and to do of his good pleasure" (Phil. 2:13). The testimony of these two passages is to the effect that there is now no such thing as an independent human life. Men are either energized by God or by Satan, and accordingly as they are saved or unsaved.

The estate of the unsaved is revealed again in Col. 1:13: "Who hath delivered us from the power of darkness, and hath translated us into the kingdom of his dear Son." Until this divine transformation is wrought, man must be considered as yet in the "powers of darkness." This revelation is given in other passages: "Jesus answered and said unto him, Verily, verily, I say unto thee, Except a man be born again, he cannot see the kingdom of God" (John 3:3); "But the natural man receiveth not the things of the Spirit of God: for they are foolishness unto him: neither can he know them, because they are spiritually discerned" (1 Cor. 2:14); "But if our gospel be hid, it is hid to them that are lost: in whom the god of this world hath blinded the minds of them which believe not, lest the light of the glorious gospel of Christ, who is the image of God, should shine unto them" (2 Cor. 4:3, 4); "We know that we are of God, and the whole world lieth in the evil one" (1 John 5:19, R.V.); "At that time ye were without Christ, being aliens from the commonwealth of Israel, and strangers from the covenants of promise, having no hope, and without God in the world" (Eph. 2:12); "Being filled with all unrighteousness, fornication, wickedness, covetousness, maliciousness; full of envy, murder, debate, deceit, malignity; whisperers, backbiters, haters of God, despiteful, proud, boasters, inventors of evil things, disobedient to parents, without understanding, covenant-breakers, without natural affection, implacable, unmerciful: who knowing the judgment of God, that they which commit such things are worthy of death, not only do the same, but have pleasure in them that do them" (Rom. 1:29-32); "As it is written, There is none righteous, no, not one: there is none that understandeth, there is none that seeketh after God. They are all gone out of the way, they are together become unprofitable; there is none that doeth good, no, not one. Their throat is an open sepulchre; with their tongues they have used deceit; the poison of asps is under their lips: whose mouth is full of cursing and bitterness: their feet are swift to shed blood: destruction and misery are in their ways: and the way of peace have they not known: there is no fear of God before their eyes" (Rom. 3:10-18); "Now the works of the flesh are manifest, which are these: Adultery, fornication, uncleanness, lasciviousness, idolatry, witchcraft, hatred, variance, emulations, wrath, strife, seditions, heresies, envyings, murders, drunkenness, revellings, and such like" (Gal. 5:19-21); "God saw that the wickedness of man was great in the earth, and that every imagination of the thoughts of his heart was only evil continually" (Gen. 6:5); "Behold, I was shapen in iniquity; and in sin did my mother conceive me" (Psa. 51:5); "The heart is deceitful above all things, and desperately wicked: who can know it?" (Jer. 17:9); "From within, out of the heart of men, proceed evil thoughts, adulteries, fornications, murders, thefts, covetousness, wickedness, deceit, lasciviousness, an evil eye, blasphemy, pride, foolishness" (Mk. 7:21, 22); "That which is born of the flesh is flesh" (John 3:6); "Because the mind of the flesh is enmity against God; for it is not subject to the law of God, neither indeed can it be" (Rom. 8:7, R.V.); "And you hath he quickened who were dead in trespasses and sins, * * * and were by nature the children of wrath even as others" (Eph. 2:1, 3); "There is not a just man upon earth, that doeth good, and sinneth not" (Ec. 7:20); "We are all as an unclean thing, and all our righteousnesses are as filthy rags" (Isa. 64:6).

After this manner the Bible reveals the present estate of the unsaved, and upon the above lines of distinction which are outside the sphere of this world. Every condition presented in these passages demands a superhuman power for its cure. Men are not said to be lost in the eyes of their fellow-men, or as measured by the standards of the institutions of the world. They are lost in the sight of a Holy God, with Whom they finally have to do, and under the conditions that exist and are effective in a larger sphere. In like manner, men are not saved by an adjustment to the estimates and conclusions of the limited world of fallen humanity, or by what may seem to them to be reasonable or unreasonable. Salvation is not a human undertaking. It did not originate in this sin-cursed world. It is of God and unto God, and hence moves along lines and under conditions and necessities which are of a higher realm. To be saved one must see himself as God sees him, and adapt himself to the divine principles of another world, which principles have been faithfully revealed in the written Word. A man of faith is one who thus adapts himself to the revelation of God; one who is instructed by and acts on the unfolding of facts revealed by God which would otherwise be unknown through human understanding.

It was this divine estimate of humanity, described by the words "lost," "perish," "condemned," "under the wrath of God," "blind," "in the powers of darkness," "dead in trespasses and sins," which brought the Saviour from heaven to earth. It was this dark picture that impelled Him to give His life a ransom for many. His saving work was a practical accomplishment. It has provided every needed cure that could be demanded by the infinite purity and holiness of God.

CHAPTER III

THE THREE-FOLD MESSAGE OF THE CROSS

The Epistle to the Hebrews opens with a reference to the messages of God which have been projected into this world, and which have widened the possible scope of man's understanding and action from the limitations of the things of this world and the conclusions of finite minds to the issues of the entire sphere of God's redemptive purposes and the verities of the Infinite. God has spoken. The effect of the message has been far reaching, men generally believe in certain facts the knowledge of which could come only from the Scriptures of Truth; but men do not always pause to consider all of God's message and its personal application to them with its necessary demands upon their faith. They believe in the Bible heaven, but do not carefully consider the only condition the Bible reveals upon which any soul can enter therein; they believe in the fact of sin, but seem to care little for the priceless cure divinely set forth for it; they believe there is a holy God and that men are sinners, but do not estimate what problems were involved in bringing about a possible reconciliation between that holy God and the meritless sinner: yet how faithfully God has spoken on all these issues! It is not enough to believe generally that God has spoken. What He has said must be carefully weighed and personally applied. His message is as a shaft of light from the eternal sphere shining into a world where sin's darkness and blindness are supreme. Happy indeed is the man who humbly receives every word God has spoken both of sin and salvation, and is thus able to look into the realms of glory along this radiant shaft of divine revelation. The following are the opening words to the letter to the Hebrews:

"God who at sundry times and in divers manners spake in time past unto the fathers by the prophets, hath in these last days spoken unto us by his Son." The message from God spoken to the fathers by the prophets is contained in the Old Testament. The message spoken to us by His Son and which was confirmed unto us by them that heard Him, is contained in the New Testament. This latter message is primarily of "So great salvation" which in no wise can be neglected with impunity.

God has disclosed His own essential being through His Son. In this revelation which He has made through His Son, God is said to be Light, Life and Love, or Wisdom, Power and Love. Christ was an outshining of these elements which are in the being of God, and that manifestation of His being through the Son was made in terms which the finite mind might grasp. Men of Christ's time, from their study of Him, were able to say: "No man ever spake as this man," and "We know that thou art a teacher come from God: for no man can do the miracles that thou doest, except God be with him." So the wisdom and power of God were recognized in Christ; but the wisdom and power of God had already a sufficient revelation in the very things that were created, so that even the heathen world is without excuse. "Because that which may be known of God is manifest in them; for God hath shewed it unto them. For the invisible things of him from the creation of the world are clearly seen, being understood by the things that are made, even his eternal power and Godhead; so that they are without excuse" (Rom. 1:19, 20).

At least three messages from God through His Son are revealed in the cross:

LOVE

In John 1:18 a special manifestation of God through the Son is mentioned: "No man hath seen God at any time; the only begotten Son, which is in the bosom of the Father, he hath declared him." "No man hath (fully) seen God at any time" would indicate that while His power and wisdom had been revealed to some extent by the things created, the complete revelation had not been given and there was to be a very special unfolding of His bosom of love. The Son was in the bosom of the Father (the seat of the affections; from that bosom He never departed). "For God so loved the world, that he gave his only begotten Son."

Every moment of the earth life of Jesus was a manifestation of God's love, but one event in the ministry of Jesus is especially designated as the means by which the bosom of God was unveiled. "Hereby perceive we the love of God, because he laid down his life for us" (1 John 3:16); "In this was manifested the love of God toward us, because that God sent his only begotten Son into the world, that we might live through him. Herein is love, not that we loved God, but that he loved us and sent his Son to be a propitiation for our sins" (1 John 4:9, 10); "But God commendeth his love toward us, in that, while we were yet sinners, Christ died for us" (Rom. 5:8). In the cross of Christ, therefore, God hath declared His love, and this declaration is addressed as a personal message to every individual. It may be concluded that when that divine message really reaches a heart that individual will thereby become conscious of a fact far beyond the range of human knowledge and so far reaching in its value that it transcends all other issues in life and death. It becomes intensely personal according to the testimony of the apostle: "Who loved me and gave himself for me." That knowledge-surpassing love is proven and expressed to "me" by the fact that He gave Himself for "me." The vital question at once becomes, what did He do for "me"? The Scriptures make it plain that He did enough to demonstrate finally and perfectly the infinite love of God. "Hereby perceive we the love of God because he laid down his life for us." This is more than a moral example: it is a distinct service rendered, and on so vast a scale that it adequately expresses the deepest message from the Father's bosom. The message must be understood by those to whom it is addressed, but not necessarily by the processes of mere human reason. The cross of Christ was the final answer to the great necessities and problems which sin had imposed on the very heart of God. This is revealed, and is knowable only to the extent to which God has spoken, and never because man has examined and analyzed the heart of the Infinite. Human philosophy and blind unbelief have woven many veils which have tended to obscure God's plain revelation. The conditions which moved the heart of God exist in the higher realm and have no comparisons or counterparts in the range of human knowledge, hence human reason cannot be deemed sufficient to judge or challenge that which God has seen fit to reveal. Anything which adequately represents the infinite love of God will hardly be compressed into the limitations of man's wisdom. It is most probable that eternity itself will prove to be but a ceaseless unfolding of that fathomless expression of boundless love. Even now that divine expression of love in the cross becomes the source of supreme ecstasy to the one who has received the message into his heart. "God forbid that I should glory, save in the cross of our Lord Jesus Christ." In striking contrast to this, the unsaved person, either Jew or Gentile, finds no attraction whatever, in the same cross. "For the preaching of the cross is to them that perish foolishness; but unto us which are saved it is the power of God."

That something of eternal value to lost humanity was accomplished in the cross is clearly revealed. Just how much was accomplished could not be fully revealed. However, some things are made plain. The eternal issue of sin was called into question at Calvary's cross, and a sufficient Substitute stood in the sinner's place until all grounds of condemnation were forever past and every righteous judgment of God was perfectly met. Human wisdom has sometimes challenged this revelation on the supposed grounds that it would be immoral for God to lay on an innocent victim the condemnation that belongs to another. This might be true if it could be discovered that the innocent One was an unwilling victim; but on this point every doubt is forever dispelled. In Heb. 10:1-14, where the sin offerings of the Old Testament are held in contrast to the one offering of Christ, the Lord is recorded as saying, "Then said I, Lo, I am come, to do thy will O God." So at the time of His crucifixion, He said to His Father: "Nevertheless not my will, but thine, be done."

But there is a still deeper truth to be considered when the challenge is made that the substitutionary death of Christ is an "immoral thing." "God was in Christ reconciling the world unto himself." Shall not the infinite God be morally free to bear on His own breast the doom of the one His infinite love would save? Would not a mother be morally justified who had flung herself between her child and the fire? Would the child be justified in later years, when gazing on those frightful scars, to deem that love-act as an immoral thing? What Christ bore we are saved from bearing. His work was effective. "He died for me": not to shew me how to die. He died that I might not die. God's love, in expressing itself to human hearts, provided a substitute for them in their sin judgments the issues of which reach out into infinity. This, we are told, is what divine love did. Who can measure the blasphemy of those who speak of this love-expression as an "immoral thing"? So fallen is the heart of unregenerate man that he will even attempt to incriminate by a charge of immorality the very God Who seeks to save him from his doom.

The cross of Christ, though unveiling the heart of God in a moment of time, was, nevertheless, the expression of that which is eternal in that heart. Christ was "a Lamb slain from the foundation of the world." What God did for sinners, therefore, is an expression of His constant attitude toward them. The cross is an assurance of the undiminished love of God at this very hour.

Only in the cross has God perfectly revealed His love to sinful man: not in nature, nor in the things and relationships of this life; for these may fail. And when they fail the stricken heart that has trusted these outward benefits alone as the evidence of God's love is heard to say, "it cannot be true that God loves me," God's perfect and final revelation of His love is in and through the cross, and the heart to whom this message has come is possessed with all the consolations of grace in the midst of the trials and afflictions of life. Such a one can say, "though He slay me yet will I trust Him." In these last days God is speaking through His Son of His personal love for each individual. Reader, has God said anything to you through His Son? Can you say in the joy of that greatest of all messages, "God forbid that I should glory, save in the cross of our Lord Jesus Christ"? If the cross has not become this to you, is it not evidence to you that you are neglecting this great salvation in spite of all professions and good intentions, and from the unhappy end of such failure there can be no escape?

SIN

While Christians are grateful to Christ for what He did in His death for them on the cross, should they not be grateful also in some degree to the Roman soldiers who put Christ to death? This question has been raised by unbelief and may well be answered by first discovering just what part the soldiers took in that great event as it is viewed in the Bible. In John 10:17, 18 we read that Jesus said: "Therefore doth my Father love me, because I lay down my life, that I might take it again. No man taketh it from me, but I lay it down of myself. I have power to lay it down, and I have power to take it again." He evidently made no resistance at the moment of His crucifixion, which was doubtless in great contrast to the violent struggles of the two thieves and wholly opposed to the highest ideal of that time when self-preservation and self-advancement were the first consideration of all men. Whatever else took place, no man took His life from Him. So, also, the last words recorded as falling from His lips on the cross were of victory and authority. "Father, into thy hands I commend (deposit) my spirit." This language distinctly indicates that His death was in no way a defeat through human force. Not one reference in the Bible, outside the mere historical statement of the crucifixion, ever assigns this death to human sources. It is rather indicated that God the Father was acting in that death.

"All we like sheep have gone astray; we have turned every one to his own way; and the LORD hath laid on him the iniquity of us all" (Isa. 53:6); "Whom God hath set forth to be a propitiation through faith in his blood" (Rom. 3:25); "For he hath made him to be sin for us, who knew no sin; that we might be made the righteousness of God in him" (2 Cor. 5:21). The soldiers might take a human life; but God alone could accomplish a reconciliation through Christ's death and thereby solve the great problems created by human sin. Christians are saved by the divine reconciliation alone, and no gratitude is due the human factors in the death of Christ.

The deed of the soldiers is not without meaning, however. From the first sin of man to the present hour every unregenerate person is said to be at enmity toward God. That enmity is usually covered and latent, but as assuredly exists as the Word of God is true. It was the will of God that at the exact time and place when and where His infinite love was being unveiled there should be an unveiling, as well, of the desperate wickedness of man. Every human act in the crucifixion was a revelation of the fallen creature; yet to crown it all, one man, as though representing a fallen race, took a spear and drove it into the heart of God. The deep significance here lies in the inexplicable fact that "God was in Christ" and that this human act was in reality against the person of God, as well as a rejection of the human presence of Christ and the blessings of grace He presented. So all those who tarry in unbelief are warned that in so doing they "crucify to themselves the Son of God afresh, and put him to an open shame."

Thus no man can be ignorant of the true nature of his own sinful heart who has honestly faced the meaning of the sin of rejecting Christ as enacted in the crucifixion. On this point God has spoken through His Son. Oh the sin of even hesitating to receive the marvels of God's grace as offered to lost men in the cross of Christ!

RIGHTEOUSNESS

The cross of Christ is also a message from God in that it is said to be a declaration of the righteousness of God. "Whom God hath set forth to be a propitiation through faith in his blood, to declare his righteousness for the remission of sins that are past, through the forbearance of God; to declare, I say, at this time his righteousness: that he might be just, and the justifier of him which believeth in Jesus" (Rom. 3:25, 26). The English word "declare," as used in this passage, is also used in the passage in John 1:18 already considered, wherein the bosom of God is said to have been "declared." The Greek words from which these two translations are made are not the same. In the passage in John the word presents the idea of announcement (cf. Lk. 24:35; Acts 10:8; 15:12, 14; 21:19), while in the passage in Romans the word indicates the legal aspect of a full proof of something in question (cf. 2 Cor. 8:24, "Proof"; Phil. 1:28, "Evident token").

In verse 25 of the passage under consideration the evident proof of the righteousness of God was made in the cross concerning the sins committed before the death of Christ. God had always anticipated a perfect and sufficient sacrifice for sin. The blood of bulls and goats had never taken away sin, but had been the divinely appointed symbol of the blood that was to be shed. In view of the sacrifice that was to be, God had passed over, or pretermitted, the sins aforetime on the condition that the offender present the symbolic innocent sacrifice for his sins. Although the offender may have comprehended but little of all the divine meaning and purpose, the sacrifice stood as a covenant with Jehovah that He would, in the fullness of time, meet all the need of the sinner. When the true and sufficient sacrifice was accomplished, that sacrifice stood as a full proof that God had been righteous in all the generations wherein He had freely acted in view of that great event which was yet to come.

In verse 26 the declaration, or full proof, of the righteousness of God is made in the cross in relation to the sins committed since the cross and in this time when the human responsibility for adjustment and cure for sin is not the providing of a symbolic sacrifice, as in the Old Testament, but is rather conditioned on a personal trust in the sufficient sacrifice fully accomplished on the cross. Such justification, according to this verse, is for "him which believeth in Jesus."

This verse also states what we may believe to be the deepest divine problem. How can the righteous God deal righteously with the sinner and at the same time satisfy His own compassion and love in saving him from the doom His own righteousness must ever impose on one who commits sin? Though He love the sinner, there are unalterable conditions to be met in upholding His justice and personal character. Sin cannot be treated otherwise than sin, else all standards of holiness and justice fail. This is not a remote and exceptional problem; but is one as far reaching and important as the very fact of the existence and destiny of the human family itself. It must also be considered as claiming the utmost attention of all intelligences of the universe. Can sin be righteously treated as sin and still a way be provided for the salvation of the sinner? Any theory which tends to lessen the imperative for judgment which was created by sin, does not fully weigh the fact of the unalterable character of the righteousness of God. Is He not all-powerful and all-sufficient and can He not waive aside the sin of those creatures His hands have made? Is He bound by any law whatsoever? The answer is not of human origin, any more than is the question, though the human mind may comprehend it. Even God cannot change the character of righteousness by altering or lessening to the slightest degree its holy demands. What is done for the satisfaction of His love in saving any whom His righteousness condemns must be done in full view of all that His righteousness could ever require. The cross is said to be the message of God through His Son in answer to this divine problem. He might not change the demands of righteousness, but He has sufficient power and resource to meet perfectly those demands for every sin-doomed soul. The dying Christ was "set forth" in order that God might be just and at the same time satisfy His heart of love in being the justifier of him which believeth in Jesus. As the righteous Judge, He pronounced the full divine sentence against sin. As the Saviour of sinners, He stepped down from His judgment throne and took into His breast the very doom He had in righteousness imposed. The cross declares the righteousness of God, and because of that cross His righteousness cannot suffer or ever be called in question, even when He wholly pardons the chief of sinners and floods him with the riches of grace. All that righteousness can demand has by the very Judge been supplied; for it was God Who was "in Christ reconciling the world unto himself." The problem was within the very nature of God Himself. How can He remain just and still justify the sinner whom He loved with an everlasting love? He was the mediator between His own righteous Being and the meritless, helpless sinner. The redemption price has been paid by the very Judge Himself.

This is revealed to finite man as being now

accomplished by the infinite God. God has not thus acted because man requested Him to do so. It was His own solution of His own problem determined by Him before any man came into being. It was made actual in the cross in "the fullness of time." Man is only asked to believe and act on the facts thus revealed. Redemption by the cross was not God's second best as contrasted with the innocency of Adam in the garden. It was in the divine councils from the foundation of the world and its accomplishment is unto a heavenly state above angels and archangels, yea, into the very image of Christ. This is the good news of the Gospel. Sin's judgments are already perfectly met. "He loved me and gave Himself for me." While the cross is to the unsaved Jew "a stumbling block" and to the unsaved Gentile "foolishness," it is to those that are saved "the power of God and the wisdom of God." These extremes in the conclusions concerning the cross by equally intelligent people can be accounted for on no other ground than that some, by the Spirit, have apprehended and accepted the declaration of God's love and righteousness which He has made in the cross. They have seen that the very power of God in saving grace has been set free, and that God's own wisdom has been disclosed in solving His own problem of saving sinners by that cross. The new song of such a heart is, "God forbid that I should glory, save in the cross of our Lord Jesus Christ, by whom the world is crucified unto me, and I unto the world." All praise be unto Him! Christ was God's Lamb "that taketh away the sin of the world." "He became a curse for us." "He bore our sins in his body on the tree." "He was made sin for us." "Jehovah hath caused to rest on him the iniquity of us all." "He is the propitiation for our sins." "He tasted death for every man."

It is, therefore, now possible for the righteous God to

deal graciously with a sinner because that sinner, through the substitutionary death of Christ, is, in the estimation of God, placed beyond his own execution, and the ground of condemnation is forever past. God has, for His own sake, removed every moral hindrance which His infinite holiness might see in sinful man, and so it is now possible for Him to exercise the last impulse of His love without reservation or limitation.

When thus unshackled and untrammeled in His love, He, through His own lavishings of love and grace, places the sinner in the eternal glory finally perfected into the very image of His Son. There is nothing in the highest heaven beyond that. It is the greatest possible thing that God can do. It is the infinite demonstration of His grace. God's grace in action is more than love. It is love operating in full recognition and adjustment to every demand of righteousness. "Even so might grace reign through righteousness unto eternal life by Jesus Christ our Lord."

The conclusion from these revelations is that by the cross God has declared our sin, His own righteousness and His own unmeasured love. He has spoken to us through His Son. The reasonable requirement is that we believe that message. This is the only condition given in the Bible upon which one may enter into God's saving grace.

CHAPTER IV

THE PRESENT VALUES OF THE CROSS TO THE UNSAVED

Every thoughtful person is compelled to assign some reason for the death of Christ. The problem consists in the fact that the sinless, harmless Man Who most evidently was able to defend Himself against all human strength, and being very God could have dismissed the universe from His presence by one word; nevertheless allowed Himself to be crucified in seeming weakness, and afterward appeared in resurrection life and power. Since both the death of Christ and His resurrection are fully established facts of history, the question demands solution. Why did He suffer Himself thus to be put to death? It is certain He did not need to die either because of His own sinfulness or weakness. This problem does not remain a mere abstract riddle. The death of Christ is explained in the Scriptures and the personal acceptance or rejection of that divine explanation is declared to be the point which determines the destiny of each individual. Men are said to stand, or fall, not by their moral, or religious standards, but by their personal choice in relation to the death and saving grace of Christ. The question is as important, therefore, as the destiny of man.

The Scriptures know but one solution to the problem

of the death of Christ -- one, and only one, whether it be in type in the Old Testament, or in the exact unfoldings of the history and doctrine of the New Testament. The Bible lends no sanction to differing human theories on this point. Such speculations are but shadows of the divine revelation and their promulgation is, like any counterfeit, a misleading substitute for the real Gospel of saving grace.

Almost every passage related to the cross could be called into evidence in determining the divine reason for the sacrifice on the part of the Son of God. In these divine records two great truths are evident: He died as a substitute for some one else, and that some one else is each and every individual in all the lost world of mankind. "But he was wounded for our transgressions, he was bruised for our iniquities: the chastisement of our peace was upon him; and with his stripes we are healed. All we like sheep have gone astray; we have turned every one to his own way; and the LORD hath laid on him the iniquity of us all" (Isa. 53:5, 6); "Behold the Lamb of God, which taketh away the sin of the world" (John 1:29); "For God so loved the world, that he gave his only begotten Son, that whosoever believeth in him should not perish, but have everlasting life" (John 3:16); "Because we thus judge, that if one died for all, then were all dead" (2 Cor. 5:14); "Who will have all men to be saved, and to come unto the knowledge of the truth" (1 Tim. 2:1); "That he by the grace of God should taste death for every man" (Heb. 2:9); "And he is the propitiation for our sins: and not for ours only, but also for the sins of the whole world" (1 John 2:2).

In the clearest terms this death is here said to be a substitution. He did not die to show men how to die gracefully, or bravely: He died that they might not die.

What He did, therefore, does not need to be done again. It is something accomplished for every person and in such perfection as to be fully satisfying to the infinite God. In like manner these passages are characterized by such universal words as "all," "every man" and "the whole world." From this it must be believed that the death of Christ has already provided a great potential and provisional value for every guilty sinner, which is now awaiting his personal recognition.

Preceding the dismissal of His spirit as He hung upon the cross Jesus said, "It is finished." This could hardly have referred to the fact that His own life or sufferings were at an end. It was rather the divine announcement of the fact that a complete transaction regarding the judgment of sin and the sufficient grounds of salvation for every sinner was accomplished. It is important to consider what, according to the Scriptures, was then finished.

To know the meaning of three Bible words which relate the cross of Christ to the sinner will throw some light upon the character and extent of the work that is said to be "finished" for the whole unsaved world.

First -- Reconciliation: This word, or the doctrine it represents, does not directly appear in the Old Testament. There the thought is always of an immediate and personal atonement by shedding of blood. In the New Testament its meaning is that of a complete and thorough change accomplished by the actual removal of the cause of enmity, so making reconciliation. The most illuminating passage on this truth is found in 2 Cor. 5:14-21 R.V. "For the love of Christ constraineth us; because we thus judge, that one died for all, therefore all died; and he died for all, that they that live should no longer live unto themselves, but unto him who for their sakes died and rose again.

Wherefore we henceforth know no man after the flesh: even though we have known Christ after the flesh, yet now we know him so no more. Wherefore if any man is in Christ, he is a new creature: the old things are passed away; behold, they are become new. But all things are of God, who reconciled us to himself through Christ, and gave unto us the ministry of reconciliation; to wit, that God was in Christ reconciling the world unto himself, not reckoning unto them their trespasses, and having committed unto us the word of reconciliation. We are ambassadors therefore on behalf of Christ, as though God were entreating by us: we beseech you on behalf of Christ, be ye reconciled to God. Him who knew no sin he made to be sin on our behalf; that we might become the righteousness of God in him."

The subsequent truth in this passage grows out of the primary statement of verse 14, wherein it is said that the death of Christ was for all, and, therefore, in a legal sense, all have died in that death. The logic is irresistible. If it be admitted that He died for all (and the Scriptures know no limitation in the universal provision in that death), then the value of that death has been secured and provided for all, and since this is an undertaking which began in the councils of God and was ordained to meet the righteous requirements of His own Being, these values have been secured on a plane which answers the highest demands of the Infinite.

That Jesus died for an individual constitutes the greatest thing that can be said of that person, and, to a truly spiritual understanding, the minor classifications of the human family cease before the overwhelming revelation. "Henceforth know we no man after the flesh." He is only to be known as one for whom Jesus died. In like manner, on the ground of the perfect divine provision and accomplishment in the cross it is added: "If any man be in Christ he is a new creature (creation): old things have passed away; behold, all things are become new. But all things are of God, who reconciled us (or thoroughly changed us in relation) to himself through Christ." The Apostle then adds, "God was in Christ reconciling the world unto himself, not reckoning unto them their trespasses." The world is thus thoroughly changed in its relation to God by the death of His Son. God Himself is not said to be changed: He has thoroughly changed the world in its relation to Himself by the death of Christ. God Himself has undertaken the needed mediation between His own righteous Person and the sinful world. The provision of a Mediator and the grounds of mediation for the whole world does not save the world, but it does render the salvation of the individual possible in the righteousness of God.

Those who are thus saved have received a ministry from God. "We are ambassadors, therefore, on behalf of Christ, as though God were entreating by us: we beseech you on behalf of Christ, be ye reconciled to God."

From this Scripture we may conclude that there is a two-fold aspect of reconciliation: first, that which God hath already wrought in" Christ by which He has thoroughly changed the relation of the whole world to Himself so that He does not reckon their trespasses unto them, and, second, a reconciliation for which we may plead and which must take place in the attitude of the unsaved individual through the revelation given to him in the Gospel concerning the sacrifice of Christ. Salvation is made to depend upon such a personal response to this appeal from God. Blessed indeed is the one who can say, "the love and grace of God, in removing forever my judgments and doom by the sacrifice of His Son, are wholly satisfying to me and I rest only in the Saviour thus given." The fact of the universal divine reconciliation may remain unappreciated and unconsidered, but when its eternal riches dawn on a sin-blinded soul that one, in his attitude and experience, is thoroughly changed toward God and finds a wholly new joy and peace through believing what God has already done in His boundless grace.

Second -- Redemption: Divine redemption, whether in the Old or the New Testament, is to deliver by paying the demands of the offended righteousness of God against sin. The price of such redemption is always blood alone. "When I see the blood, I will pass over you" (Ex. 12:13); "It is the blood that maketh an atonement for the soul" (Lev. 17:11); "This is my blood of the new testament, which is shed for many for the remission of sins" (Mt. 26:28); "Ye were not redeemed with corruptible things * * * but with the precious blood of Christ" (1 Pet. 1:18); "The blood of Jesus Christ his Son cleanseth us from all sin" (1 John 1:7); "Thou wast slain, and hath redeemed us to God by thy blood" (Rev. 5:9).

The full redemption by blood has been paid in the death of Christ and so in a provisional way has affected the estate of the whole world. "Who gave himself a ransom for all, to be testified in due time" (1 Tim. 2:6); "Even the Son of Man came not to be ministered unto, but to minister, and to give his life a ransom for many" (Mt. 20:28); "Behold the Lamb of God, which taketh away the sin of the world" (John 1:29).

Redemption is also by power. This was seen in the redemption of Israel from Egypt and is equally true of all redemption. The price may be paid for the slave, but he must be taken out of the slave position and set free. This is individual and such redemption by blood and power is the blessed experience of all who put their trust in the divine Redeemer.

Forgiveness, which in the Scriptures is individual, is made possible through the blood of redemption. "The priest shall make an atonement for his sin that he hath committed, and it shall be forgiven him" (Lev. 4:35); "This is my blood of the new testament, which is shed for many for the remission of sins" (Mt. 26:28); "Without shedding of blood is no remission" (Heb. 9:22); "In whom we have redemption through his blood, the forgiveness of sins" (Eph. 1:7).

Redemption, then, may also be considered in these two aspects: that which has been already accomplished through the blood of the cross, and that which may yet be done for the one who believes, through the immediate power of God. The ransom price has been paid for all; yet for the one who believes there is a further work of redemption which is manifested in the transforming and sanctifying power of the Spirit.

Happy is the individual who believes what God has written, and rests in the redeeming work of Christ as his only deliverance from the hopeless estate of the lost.

Third -- Propitiation: The meaning of this word is inexpressibly sweet. It refers to a divinely provided place of meeting, a place of propitiation. The mercy-seat of the Old Testament is spoken of in Heb. 9:5 as a place of propitiation. There, covering the broken law, was the blood-sprinkled mercy-seat, and there was the Shekinah light which spoke of the presence of God. There, too, because of the blood and what it typified, a holy God could meet a sinful man without judgments and, in turn, a sinful man could meet a holy God without dread or fear. So we find in Rom. 3:25, 26, that Christ was "set forth" by His Father God to be a propitiation through faith in His blood. So, also, in 1 John 2:2, "And he is the propitiation for our sins: and not for ours only, but for the sins of the whole world." The very blood-sprinkled body of the Son of God on the cross has become the divinely provided place of meeting where now a guilty sinner can come to God without fear, and the righteous God can receive that soul apart from all judgments and condemnation.

The publican who went up to the temple to pray, according to Lk. 18:9-14, would not so much as lift up his eyes to heaven, but smote on his breast, and said: "God be thou propitiated to me the sinner." The significance of the Greek text is not "God be merciful to me a sinner," but is more correctly expressed by the R.V. marginal rendering, "God be propitiated to me the sinner." There is a most vital distinction here. It is one thing to call on God for an exercise of immediate mercy: it is quite another thing to ask to be covered by atoning blood. How different the issue is before the unsaved now since the atoning blood has been shed! Certainly it is not a matter with them of securing some special leniency from God: it is rather a matter of believing that every needed grace has been already exercised. On the ground of a divinely provided propitiation the publican went down to his house justified, which was vastly more than being forgiven. In like manner, every soul has been as freely justified who has believed. It is a question of intelligently electing to receive and stand in the saving work of Christ which is simply to receive the Christ as a personal Saviour. The sinner thus acknowledges Christ as the divinely appointed propitiation and there in confidence rests his case before the righteous throne of God.

From these three Bible words we may conclude that there is a work now fully accomplished in the cross for every unsaved person. Such have been thoroughly changed in their relation to God by His great act of reconciliation, and He is said to be waiting for them to be thoroughly changed by the message of the Cross in reconciliation toward Him. He has redeemed them by the blood of Christ Who was "the Lamb of God that taketh away the sin of the world," but is now awaiting their act of faith toward the Christ that He might with the power of the Spirit transform them into the very sons of God. He has been propitiated toward "the whole world," but must await the willingness of the individual to stand only on the fact that the righteous judgments for sin have already been accomplished in the cross of Christ. That cross was a propitiation toward God; a reconciliation toward man; and a redemption toward sin. And this in relation to every member of the fallen human race. If men go to perdition it will be because every possible mercy from God has been resisted.

"God so loved the world that he gave his only begotten Son" -- this much is universal and so is true of all -- "that whosoever believeth in him should not perish but have everlasting life" -- is individual and personal. No one is saved by these universal things alone; but because of these universal things any one who believes may be saved. To every unsaved person, therefore, the message may be given in the full confidence in its truth that God has already completed the grounds of salvation, and they are but to believe on Him through Whom all this grace has been so perfectly wrought.

CHAPTER V

THE ONE CONDITION OF SALVATION

Notwithstanding all that has been divinely accomplished for the unsaved, they are not saved by it alone. Salvation is an immediate display of the power of God within the lifetime and experience of the individual, and is easily distinguished from those potential accomplishments finished nearly two thousand years ago in the cross. As has been stated, salvation is a work of God for man, rather than a work of man for God. No aspect of salvation, according to the Bible, is made to depend, even in the slightest degree, on human merit or works. Great stress is laid on the value of good works which grow out of a saved life, but they do not precede salvation or form any part of a basis for it. It, therefore, is revealed that the first issue between God and an unsaved person in this age is that of receiving Christ, rather than that of improving the manner of life, however urgent such improvement may be. This insistence seems to mere human reason to be an indirect, if not aimless, means of obtaining the moral improvement of men. The need of moral improvement is most evident, and simply to try to help men to be better would seem to be the direct and logical thing to do. However, the divine program strikes deeper and purposes a new creation out from which good works can flow and apart from which there can be no acceptable works in the sight of God. Unsaved men are thus shut up to the one condition upon which God can righteously make them to be new creatures in Christ Jesus.

With regard to the necessity of a new creation the unregenerate are blind in their minds (2 Cor. 4:3, 4). So also about this need a multitude of professing Christians are poorly taught, resulting in a well nigh universal misconception of the demands of the gospel. When dealing with the unsaved, false issues are often raised and these unscriptural demands appear in many forms. Satan's ministers are said to be the ministers of righteousness (2 Cor. 11:14, 15). They waive aside the Bible emphasis on a new birth, which is by the power of God through faith and which is the only source from which works acceptable to God can be produced, and devote their energy to the improvement, morally and righteously, of the individual's character. Such

workers, in spite of their sincerity and humanitarian motives, are by the Spirit of God said to be "the ministers of Satan."

The fact that the unregenerate are blinded by Satan in regard to the true gospel of grace is the explanation of the age-long plea of the moralist: "If I do the best I can God must be satisfied with that, else He is unreasonable." Granting that anyone has ever done his best, it would still be most imperfect as compared with the infinite holiness of God. God cannot, under any conditions, call that perfect which is imperfect, and He is far from unreasonable in demanding a perfect righteousness, impossible to man, while He stands ready to provide as a gift all that His holiness requires. This is exactly the offer of the Gospel. The Scriptures do not call on men of this age to present their own righteousness to God; but invite unrighteous men to receive the very righteousness of God which may be theirs through a vital union with Christ. The appeal is not self-improvement in the important matters of daily life, but that "the gift of God which is eternal life through Jesus Christ our Lord" might be received. When this eternal issue is met the more temporal matters of conduct are urged; but only on the grounds of the fact that divine salvation has been wrought for sinful man wholly apart from his own works.

The question confronting each individual, therefore, is that of the basis upon which this new creation can be gained. In such an undertaking man is powerless. All his ability must be forever set aside. It must be accomplished for him, and God alone can do it. He alone can form a new creation; He alone can deal with sin; He alone can bestow a perfect righteousness; He alone can translate from the powers of darkness into the kingdom of His dear Son.

If it were only a question of power to transform men the creative power of God has always been sufficient; but there was a greater difficulty caused by the fact of sin. Sin must first be judged, and no favor or grace can be divinely exercised until every offense of righteousness has been fully met. God cannot look on sin with the least degree of allowance, and so He can grant His favor only by and through the cross wherein, and only wherein, the consequences of sin have been forever met in His sight. Thus salvation can be accomplished, even by the infinite God, only through Jesus Christ. Hence it is that a simple trust in the Saviour opens the way into the infinite power and grace of God. It is "unto every one that believeth," "For there is none other name under heaven given among men whereby we must be saved."

This one word "believe" represents all a sinner can do and all a sinner must do to be saved. It is believing the record God has given of His Son. In this record it is stated that He has entered into all the needs of our lost condition and is alive from the dead to be a living Saviour to all who put their trust in Him. It is quite possible for any intelligent person to know whether he has placed such confidence in the Saviour. Saving faith is a matter of personal consciousness. "I know whom I have believed." To have deposited one's eternal welfare in the hands of another is a decision of the mind so definite that it can hardly be confused with anything else. On this deposit of oneself into His saving grace depends one's eternal destiny. To add, or subtract, anything from this sole condition of salvation is most perilous. The Gospel is thus often misstated in various and subtle ways. The more common of these should be mentioned specifically:

First, The unsaved are sometimes urged to pray and hope for an attitude of leniency on the part of God toward their sins: whereas they should be urged to believe that every aspect of favor and expression of love has already been wrought out by God Himself. They are not believing God when they beseech Him to be reconciled to them, when He is revealed as having already accomplished a reconciliation. The Gospel does not inspire a hope that God will be gracious: it discloses the good news that He has been gracious and challenges every man but to believe it. A criminal pleading for mercy before a judge is not in the same position as a criminal believing and rejoicing in the assurance that a full pardon is granted and that he can never be brought again into judgment.

Second, It is a most serious error to intrude any form of human works into a situation wherein God alone can work. People are sometimes led to believe that there is saving value in some public confession of Christ, or profession of a decision. "With the heart man believeth unto righteousness." This is salvation. "With the mouth confession is made unto salvation." This is the voice of the new-born child speaking to and of its Father. The only condition on which one may be saved is to believe.

Third, It is equally as great an error to give the unsaved the impression that there is saving virtue in promising to try to "lead a Christian life." No unregenerate mind is prepared to deal with the problems of true Christian living. These problems anticipate the new dynamic of the imparted divine nature, and could produce nothing but hopeless discouragement when really contemplated by an unregenerate person. There is danger, as well, that by forcing the issues of future conduct into the question the main issue of receiving Christ as Saviour may be submerged in some difficulty related to the proposed standards of living. There is an advantage in a general morality, "Sabbath observance," temperance and attendance on public and private worship; but there is no saving value in any, or all, of them. It is true that a person who enters into these things might be more apt to hear the saving Gospel of grace than otherwise; but on the other hand, the sad fact is that these very things are often depended upon by the religiously inclined to commend themselves to God. A clear distinction is found in the Bible between conversion and salvation. The former is there found to indicate no more than the humanly possible act of turning about, while the latter refers to that display of the power of God which is manifested in the whole transformation of saving grace.

Fourth, A person is not saved because he prays. Multitudes of people pray who are not saved. Praying is not believing on the Lord Jesus Christ; though the new attitude of belief may be expressed in prayer. "Without faith it is impossible to please God." In no Scripture is salvation conditioned on asking or praying. It is faith in the Saviour Who gave His precious blood a ransom for all. The publican, living and praying before the cross, pleads that God would be propitiated to him a sinner. The issue now can only be one of believing that God has been so propitiated.

Fifth, No person is now required to "seek the Lord." In Isa. 55:6 it is said to Israel, "Seek ye the LORD while he may be found," but in the New Testament relationship we are told to believe that the "Son of man is come to seek and to save that which was lost."

Sixth, It is an error to require repentance as a preliminary act preceding and separate from believing. Such insistence is too often based on Scripture which is addressed to the covenant people, Israel. They, like Christians, being covenant people, are privileged to return to God on the grounds of their covenant by repentance. There is much Scripture both in the Old Testament and in the New that calls that one nation to its long-predicted repentance, and it is usually placed before them as a separate unrelated act that is required. The preaching of John the Baptist, of Jesus and the early message of the disciples was, "repent for the kingdom of heaven is at hand"; but it was addressed only to Israel (Mt. 10:5, 6). This appeal was continued to that nation even after the day of Pentecost or so long as the Gospel was preached to Israel alone (Acts 2:38; 3:19. See also 5:31). Paul mentions also a separate act of repentance in the experience of Christians (2 Cor. 7:8-11. See also Rev. 2:5).

The conditions are very different, however, in the case

of an unsaved Gentile, who is a "stranger to the covenants of promise, having no hope, and without God in the world," and equally different for any individual Jew in this age. In presenting the Gospel to these classes there are one hundred and fifteen passages at least wherein the word "believe" is used alone and apart from every other condition as the only way of salvation. In addition to this there are upwards of thirty-five passages wherein its synonym "faith" is used. There are but six passages addressed to unsaved Gentiles wherein repentance appears either alone or in combination with other issues. These are: God "now commandeth all men everywhere to repent" (Acts 17:30); "Repent and turn to God" (Acts 26:20); "Repentance unto life" (Acts 11:18); "Repentance and faith" (Acts 20:21); "The goodness of God that leadeth to repentance" (Rom. 2:4); "All should come to repentance" (2 Pet. 3:9). That repentance is not saving is evidenced in the case of Judas, who repented and yet went to perdition. It is worthy of note that there are twenty-five passages wherein "believe," or "faith," is given as the only condition of Gentile salvation to one passage wherein repentance appears for any reason whatsoever. It would seem evident from this fact that repentance, like all other issues, is almost universally omitted from the great salvation passages, that such repentance as is possible to an unsaved person in this dispensation is included in the one act of believing. The statement in 1 Thes. 1:9, 10 may serve as an illustration. Here it is said: "Ye turned to God from idols to serve the living and true God; and to wait for his Son from heaven." This represents one all-inclusive act. Such is the accuracy of the Bible. Had the record been that they turned from idols to God, the act of turning from idols would have stood alone as a preliminary undertaking and would suggest a separate work of repentance. In Acts 11:21 it is stated that many "believed and turned to God."

This is not difficult to understand. The born-again person might thus turn to God after believing; but there is no revelation that God is expecting works meet for anything from that which He has termed to be dead in trespasses and sins.

To believe on Christ is to see and believe the all-sufficiency of His saving grace. This most naturally includes abandoning all other grounds of hope, and the experiencing of such sorrow for sin as would lead one to claim such a Saviour. It is doubtful if the sinner of "this present evil age" can produce greater sorrow than this, and of what avail would greater sorrow be? No estimate is possible of the wrong that has been done in demanding the unsaved of this age to experience some particular degree of sorrow for sin, over which they could have no control, before they could be assured that the way was open for them to God. Multitudes have been driven into unrealities or into hopeless doubt as they have thus groped in darkness. The good news of the Gospel does not invite men to any sorrow whatsoever, or to works of repentance alone: it invites them to find immediate "joy and peace in believing." Repentance, according to the Bible, is a complete change of mind and, as such, is a vital element in saving faith; but it should not now be required, as a separate act, apart from saving faith.

The Biblical emphasis upon Gentile repentance or any repentance in this age will be more evident when the full meaning of the word "believe" is understood.

Seventh, Moreover, no Scripture requires confession of sin as a condition of salvation in this age. A regenerate person who has wandered from fellowship may return to his place of blessing by a faithful confession of his sin. 1 John 1:9 is addressed only to believers. "If we confess our sins, he is faithful and just to forgive us our sins, and to cleanse us from all unrighteousness." The unsaved person must come to God by faith. "For by grace are ye saved through faith" (Eph. 2:8). Believing is related in the Bible to two other actions: "Hear and believe" (Acts 15:7; Rom. 10:14); "Believe and be baptized" (Acts 8:13; Mk. 16:16 R.V.). In the latter passage it may be noted that baptism is not mentioned when the statement is repeated in the negative form. "He that believeth and is baptized shall be saved; and he that disbelieveth shall be condemned." The unsaved person is condemned for not believing rather than for not being baptized. Thus believing here, as everywhere, is the only condition of salvation.

The far-reaching importance of believing may also be seen in the fact that men are said to be lost in this age because they do not believe. "He that believeth on him is not condemned: but he that believeth not is condemned already, because he hath not believed on the name of the only begotten Son of God" (John 3:18). "He that disbelieveth shall be condemned" (Mk. 16:16 R.V.). Likewise when the Spirit is said to approach the unsaved to convince them of sin, He is not said to make them conscious or ashamed of their personal transgressions. One sin only is mentioned: "Of sin, because they believe not on me" (John 16:9). "This is the condemnation, that light is come into the world, and men loved darkness rather than light, because their deeds were evil" (John 3:19). The sin sacrifice of the cross is forever satisfying to God. What God does is based on His own estimate of the finished work of Christ. The facts and conditions of salvation are based on that divine estimate rather than upon the estimate of men. That men are not now condemned primarily because of the sins which Christ has borne is finally stated in 2 Cor. 5:14, 19 R.V.: "We thus judge, that if one died for all, therefore all died"; "God was in Christ reconciling the world unto himself, not reckoning unto them their trespasses." The greatest problem for the infinite God was to provide the reconciliation of the cross: the greatest problem for man is simply to believe the record in its fullness. To reject the Saviour is not only to refuse the gracious love of God, but is to elect, so far as one can do, to remain under the full guilt of every sin as though no Saviour had been provided, or no sacrifice had been made. No more terrible sin can be conceived of than the sin of rejecting Christ. It gathers into itself the infinite crime of despising the divine mercy and grace, and, in intent, assumes the curse of every transgression before God. Thus men are electing to stand in their own sins before God. It will be seen that this personal choice becomes a part of the final judgment of those who believe not. Jesus said: "If ye believe not that I am he, ye shall die in your sins" (John 8:24). At the judgment of the wicked dead before the Great White Throne, those standing there are said to be judged "according to their works." There is additional evidence recorded against them at that judgment seat: their names are not written in the Lamb's book of life. This might be taken as evidence that they have rejected the "Lamb of God that taketh away the sin of the world." It should be added that it was the divine program in this age that the Gospel should be preached to every creature. And thus every person should have heard and either accepted or rejected the message of Grace. God alone can righteously judge those who have never heard because of the failure of His messengers.

The Apostle John in his Gospel uses the word "believe" in its various forms about eighty-six times and never related to repentance or human works and merit.

This Gospel, which so clearly states the present way of life, is said to be written for a definite purpose: "But these are written that ye might believe that Jesus is the Christ, the Son of God; and that believing ye might have life through his name."

CHAPTER VI

THE RICHES OF GRACE IN CHRIST JESUS

In considering the Bible doctrine of salvation it is important to distinguish between those things which have already been done for all, and those things which are done for the individual at the instant he believes. The sum total of that which has been done for both classes constitutes "the riches of grace in Christ Jesus." But the things divinely accomplished at the instant of believing alone form that aspect of salvation which is already accomplished in and for the one who believes. This is salvation in its past tense aspect, i. e., salvation from the guilt, penalty and condemnation of sin. This portion of the doctrine of salvation, like the other tense aspects, includes only what God is said to do for man, and nothing whatsoever that man is said to do for God, or for himself. There is an important distinction to be made, as well, between the drawing, convincing work of the Spirit for the unsaved when He convinces of sin, righteousness and judgment, and "the things that accompany salvation." The former is the work of God in bringing the unsaved who are blinded by Satan (2 Cor. 4:3, 4) to an intelligent decision for Christ; the latter is the outworking of that salvation after they believe. So, also, there is a difference to be noted between the work of God in the past tense aspect of salvation and the growth and development of the one who is thus saved. He is to "grow in grace and in the knowledge of our Lord and Saviour Jesus Christ." He is to be "changed from glory to glory." These, too, are divine undertakings for the individual, and are in no way a part of that which is wrought of God the moment one believes.

Most of the great doctrinal epistles of the New Testament may be divided into a general two-fold division: namely, first, that which represents the work of God already accomplished for the believer, and, second, that which represents the life and work of the believer for God. The first eight chapters of Romans contain the whole doctrine of salvation in its past and present tense aspects: the last section, beginning with chapter twelve (chapters nine to eleven being parenthetical in the present purpose of God for Israel) is an appeal to the saved one to live as it becomes one thus saved. This section opens with the words, "I beseech you therefore, brethren, by the mercies of God, that ye present your bodies a living sacrifice, holy, acceptable unto God, which is your reasonable service." Such a manner of life is naturally to be expected from the one who has been divinely changed. It is a "reasonable service." So the entire closing section of Romans is an exhortation to that manner of life befitting one who is saved.

The first three chapters of Ephesians present the work of God for the individual in bringing him to his exalted heavenly position in Christ Jesus. Not one exhortation will be found in this section. The helpless sinner could do nothing to further such an undertaking. The last section, beginning with chapter 4, is altogether an appeal for a manner of life befitting one raised to such an exalted heavenly position. The first verse, as in the opening words of the hortatory section of Romans, is an epitome of all that follows: "I therefore, the prisoner of the Lord, beseech you that ye walk worthy of the vocation wherewith ye are called."

The first two chapters of Colossians reveal the glory of the Son of God and the believer's present position as identified with Him in resurrection life. This is followed by the two closing chapters, which are an appeal that may again be briefly condensed into the first two verses of the section: "If ye then be risen with Christ, seek those things which are above."

It is important to note the divine order in presenting these most vital issues. The positions to which the believer is instantly lifted by the power and grace of God are always mentioned first and without reference to any human merit or promises. Following this is the injunction for a consistent life in view of the divine blessing.

It is obvious that no attempt to imitate this manner of life could result in such exalted positions; but the positions, when wrought of God, create an entirely new demand in life and conduct (in the Word of God these demands are never laid upon unregenerate men). Such is always the order in grace. First, the unmerited divine blessing; then the life lived in the fullness of power which that blessing provides. Under the law varying blessings were given at the end according to the merit: under grace full measure of transformation is bestowed at the beginning and there follows an appeal for a consistent daily life. It is the divine purpose that a Christian's conduct should be inspired by the fact that he is already saved and blessed with all the riches of grace in Christ Jesus, rather than by the hope that an attempted imitation of the Christian standard of conduct will result in salvation.

In turning to the Scriptures to discover what it has pleased God to reveal of His saving work in the individual at the instant he believes, it will be found that there are at least thirty-three distinct positions into which such an one is instantly brought by the sufficient operation of the infinite God. All of these transformations are superhuman, and, taken together, form that part of salvation which is already the portion of every one who has believed. Of these thirty-three positions at least five important things may be said:

First, They are not experienced. They are facts of the newly created life out of which most precious experiences may grow. For example, justification is never experienced; yet it is a new eternal fact of divine life and relationship to God. A true Christian is more than a person who feels or acts on a certain high plane: he is one who, because of a whole inward transformation, normally feels and acts in all the limitless heavenly association with his Lord.

Second, The Christian positions are not progressive. They do not grow, or develop, from a small beginning. They are as perfect and complete the instant they are possessed as they ever will be in the ages to come. To illustrate, sonship does not grow into fuller sonship, even though a son may be growing. An old man is no more the son of his earthly father at the day of his death than he was at the day of his birth.

Third, These positions are in no way related to human merit. It was while we were yet sinners that Christ died for the ungodly. There is a legitimate distinction to be made between good sons and bad sons; but both equally possess sonship if they are sons at all. God is said to chasten His own because they are sons, but certainly not that they may become sons. Human merit must be excluded. It cannot be related to these divine transformations of grace; nor could they abide eternally the same if depending by the slightest degree on the finite resources. They are made to stand on the unchanging Person and merit of the eternal Son of God. There are other and sufficient motives for Christian conduct than the effort to create such eternal facts of the divine life. The Christian is "accepted (now and forever) in the beloved."

Fourth, Every position is eternal by its very nature. The imparted life of God is as eternal in its character as its Fountain Head. Hence the Word of His grace: "I give unto them eternal life and they shall never perish." The consciousness and personal realization of such relationship to God may vary with the daily walk of the believer; but the abiding facts of the new being are never subject to change in time or eternity.

Fifth, These positions are known only through a divine revelation. They defy human imagination, and since they cannot be experienced their reality can be entered into only by believing the Word of God. These eternal riches of grace are for the lowest sinner who will only believe.

That God may in some measure be glorified, some, if not all, of these positions are here given. "The half has never been told." The reader is humbly invited to remember that these things are now true of each one who believes, and if there should be the slightest doubt as to whether he has believed that question can be forever settled even before the following pages are read:

I. In the Eternal Plan of God:
1. Foreknown, "For whom he did foreknow, he also did predestinate to be conformed to the image of his Son" (Rom. 8:29. See also 1 Pet. 1:2).

2. Elect, "Knowing, brethren beloved, your election of God" (1 Thes. 1:4. See also 1 Pet. 1:2; Rom. 8:33; Col. 3:12; Tit. 1:1).

3. Predestinated, "Being predestinated according to the purpose of him who worketh all things after the council of his own will" (Eph. 1:11; Rom. 8:29, 30; Eph. 1:5).

4. Chosen, "For many are called, but few are chosen" (Mt. 22:14; 1 Pet. 2:4).

5. Called, "Faithful is he that calleth you" (1 Thes. 5:24, etc.).

II. Reconciled:

1. Reconciled by God, "And all things are of God, who hath reconciled us to himself by Jesus Christ" (2 Cor. 5:18, 19; Col. 1:20).

2. Reconciled to God, "Much more being reconciled to God" (Rom. 5:10; 2 Cor. 5:20).

III. Redeemed:

1. Redeemed by God, "In whom we have redemption through his blood" (Col. 1:14; 1 Pet. 1:18; Rom. 3:24, etc.).

2. Out of all condemnation, "There is therefore now no condemnation to them which are in Christ Jesus" (Rom. 8:1; John 5:24; 1 Cor. 11:32; John 3:18).

IV. Related to God Through a Propitiation:

1. "And he is the propitiation for our sins: and not for our's only, but also for the sins of the whole world" (1 John 2:2; Rom. 3:25, 26).

V. All Sins Covered By Atoning Blood:

1. "Who his own self bare our sins in his body on the tree" (1 Pet. 2:24; Rom. 4:25, etc.).

VI. Vitally Conjoined to Christ for Judgment of the "Old Man" Unto a New Walk:

1. "Crucified with Christ," "Knowing this, that our old man was crucified with him" (Rom. 6:6).

2. "Dead with Christ," "Now if we be dead with Christ" (Rom. 6:8); "We being dead to sin" (1 Pet. 2:24).

3. "Buried with him," "Therefore we are buried with him by baptism into death" (Rom. 6:4; Col. 2:12).

4. Raised with Christ to walk by a new life principle, "That like as Christ was raised up from the dead by the glory of the Father, even so we also should walk in newness of life" (Rom. 6:4; Col. 3:1).

VII. Free from the Law:

1. "Dead," "Wherefore, my brethren, ye also are dead to the law by

the body of Christ" (Rom. 7:4).

2. "Delivered," "Now we are delivered from the law" (Rom. 7:6; Gal. 3:25; Rom. 6:14; 2 Cor. 3:11).

VIII. Children of God:

1. "Born again," "Ye must be born again" (John 3:7; 1:12; 1 Pet. 1:23).

2. "Quickened," or made alive, "And you hath he quickened, who were dead in trespasses and sins" (Eph. 2:1; Col. 2:13).

3. "Sons of God," "Beloved, now are we the sons of God" (1 John 3:3; 2 Cor. 6:18; Gal. 3:26).

4. "A new creation," "If any man be in Christ, he is a new creature" (creation) (2 Cor. 5:17; Gal. 6:15; Eph. 2:10).

5. "Regeneration," "But according to his mercy he saved us, by the washing of regeneration, and renewing of the Holy Ghost" (Tit. 3:5; John 13:10; 1 Cor. 6:11).

IX. Adopted (placed as adult sons):

1. "Ye have received the Spirit of adoption" (Rom. 8:15, etc. So, also, a future adoption, see Rom. 8:23, etc.).

X. Acceptable to God by Jesus Christ:

1. "Made the righteousness of God in him," "Even the righteousness of God which is by faith of Jesus Christ unto all and upon all them that believe" (Rom. 3:22; 1 Cor. 1:30; 2 Cor. 5:21; Phil. 3:9).

2. Sanctified positionally, "Christ Jesus, who is made unto us * * * sanctification" (1 Cor. 1:30; 6:11). This is in no way to be confused with experimental sanctification as mentioned in John 17:17, or the final perfection of the believer (Eph. 5:27; 1 John 3:3).

3. "Perfected for ever," "For by one offering he hath perfected forever them that are sanctified" (Heb. 10:14).

4. "Made accepted in the Beloved" (Eph. 1:6; 1 Pet. 2:5).

5. "Made Meet," "Giving thanks to the Father, which hath made us meet to be partakers of the inheritance of the saints in light" (Col. 1:12).

XI. Justified:

1. "Therefore being justified by faith" (Rom. 5:1; 3:24; 8:30; 1 Cor. 6:11; Tit. 3:7).

XII. Forgiven All Trespass:

1. "In whom we have redemption through his blood, even the forgiveness of sins" (Col. 1:14; 2:13; 3:13; Eph. 1:7; 4:32. A distinction is necessary here between the complete and abiding

judicial forgiveness and the oft-repeated forgiveness within the family of God. See 1 John 1:9).

XIII. Made Nigh:

1. "But now in Christ Jesus ye who sometimes were far off are made nigh by the blood of Christ" (Eph. 2:13. With this there is a corresponding experience; see Jas. 4:8; Heb. 10:22).

XIV. Delivered from the Powers of Darkness:

1. "Who hath delivered us from the powers of darkness" (Col. 1:13; 2:13-15).

XV. Translated into the Kingdom:

1. "And hath translated us into the kingdom of his dear Son" (Col. 1:13).

XVI. On the Rock Christ Jesus:

1. "For other foundation can no man lay than that is laid, which is Jesus Christ" (1 Cor. 3:11; Eph. 2:20; 2 Cor. 1:21).

XVII. A Gift from God to Christ:

1. "I have manifested thy name unto the men which thou gavest me out of the world: thine they were, and thou gavest them me" (John 17:6, 11, 12, 20; John 10:29).

XVIII. Circumcised in Christ:

1. "In whom also ye are circumcised with the circumcision made without hands, in putting off of the body of the sins of the flesh by the circumcision of Christ" (Col. 2:11; Phil. 3:3; Rom. 2:29).

XIX. Partakers of the Holy and Royal Priesthood:

1. "Holy priesthood," "Ye also, as lively stones, are built up a spiritual house, an holy priesthood" (1 Pet. 2:5).

2. "Royal priesthood," "But ye are * * * a royal priesthood" (1 Pet. 2:9; Rev. 1:6).

XX. A Chosen Generation and a Peculiar People:

1. "But ye are a chosen generation, * * * a peculiar people" (1 Pet. 2:9; Tit. 2:14).

XXI. Having Access to God:

1. "For through him we both have access by one Spirit unto the Father" (Eph. 2:18; Rom. 5:2; Heb. 4:14-16; 10:19, 20).

XXII. Within the "Much More" Care of God (Rom. 5:9, 10):

1. Objects of His love, "But God, who is rich in mercy, for his great love wherewith he loved us" (Eph. 2:4; 5:2, etc.).

2. Objects of His grace,

a) For salvation, "For by grace are ye saved" (Eph. 2:8).

b) For keeping, "By whom also we have access by faith into this grace wherein we stand" (Rom. 5:2).

c) For service, "But to every one of us is this grace given" (Eph. 2:7).

d) For instruction, "For the grace of God that bringeth salvation hath appeared to all men, teaching us that, denying ungodliness and worldly lusts, we should live soberly, righteously, and godly, in this present age" (Tit. 2:12, 13).

3. Objects of His power, "And what is the exceeding greatness of his power to us-ward" (Eph. 1:19; Phil. 2:13).

4. Objects of His faithfulness, "For he hath said, I will never leave thee, nor forsake thee" (Heb. 13:5; Phil. 1:6).

5. Objects of His peace, "And let the peace of God rule in your hearts, to the which ye are called in one body" (Col. 3:15).

6. Objects of His consolation, "Our Father which hath loved us, and hath given us everlasting consolation" (2 Thes. 2:16).

7. Objects of His intercession, "Seeing he ever liveth to make intercession for them" (Heb. 7:25; Rom. 8:34; Heb. 9:24).

XXIII. His Inheritance:

1. "That ye may know what is the hope of his calling, and what the riches of the glory of his inheritance in the saints" (Eph. 1:18).

XXIV. Our Inheritance:

1. "An inheritance incorruptible, and undefiled, and that fadeth not away, reserved in heaven for you" (1 Pet. 1:4; Eph. 1:14; Col. 3:24; Heb. 9:15).

XXV. A Heavenly Association (Eph. 2:6):

1. Partners with Christ in life, "When Christ, who is our life, shall appear" (Col. 3:4; 1 John 5:11, 12, etc.).

2. Partners with Christ in position, "And hath raised us up together, and made us sit together in the heavenly in Christ Jesus" (Eph. 2:6).

3. Partners with Christ in service, "God is faithful, by whom ye were called into fellowship (partnership) with his Son Jesus Christ our Lord" (1 Cor. 1:9); "Workers together with God" (1 Cor. 3:9); "Workers together with him" (2 Cor. 6:1); "Ambassadors" (2 Cor. 5:20); "Ministers of God" (2 Cor. 6:4); "Ministers of the New Testament" (2 Cor. 3:6); "Epistles" (2 Cor. 3:3).

4. Partners with Christ in suffering, "If we suffer, we shall also reign with him" (2 Tim. 2:12; Phil. 1:29; 1 Pet. 2:20; 4:12, 13; 1 Thes. 3:3; Rom. 8:18; Col. 1:24).

5. Partners with Christ in betrothal, "That I may present you a

chaste virgin to Christ" (2 Cor. 11:2; Eph. 5:25-27).

XXVI. Heavenly Citizens:

1. "For our citizenship is in heaven" (Phil. 3:20, R.V.; Eph. 2:19; Heb. 12:22; Lk. 10:20).

XXVII. Of the Family and Household of God:

1. "Fellow citizens with the saints, and of the household of God" (Eph. 2:19; 3:15; Gal. 6:10).

XXVIII. Light in the Lord:

1. "Now are ye light in the Lord" (Eph. 5:8; 1 Thes. 5:4).

XXIX. Vitally United to the Father, Son, and Spirit:

1. "In God" (1 Thes. 1:1).

2. "In Christ" (John 14:20).

a) A member in His body (1 Cor. 12:13).

b) A branch in the Vine (John 15:5).

c) A stone in the building (Eph. 2:19-22).

d) A sheep in His flock (John 10:27-29).

e) A part of His bride (Eph. 5:25-27).

f) A priest of the kingdom of priests (1 Pet. 2:5, 9).

g) A saint of the "new generation" (1 Pet. 2:9).

3. "In the Spirit" (Rom. 8:9).

XXX. Blessed with the "First Fruits" and the "Earnest" of the Spirit:

1. "Born of the Spirit" (John 3:6, etc.).

2. "Baptized with the Spirit," "For by one Spirit are we all baptized into one body" (1 Cor. 12:13; 10:17).

3. Indwelt by the Spirit. "What? Know ye not that your body is the temple of the Holy Ghost which is in you, which ye have of God, and ye are not your own" (1 Cor. 6:19; 2:12; John 7:39; Rom. 5:5; 8:9; 2 Cor. 1:21; Gal. 4:6; 1 John 3:24).

4. "Sealed by the Spirit," "And grieve not the holy Spirit of God, whereby ye are sealed unto the day of redemption" (Eph. 4:30; 2 Cor. 1:22).

XXXI. Glorified:

1. "And whom he justified, them he also glorified" (Rom. 8:30).

XXXII. Complete in Him:

1. "And ye are complete in him, which is the head of all principality and power" (Col. 2:10).

XXXIII. Possessing Every Spiritual Blessing:

1. "Blessed be the God and Father of our Lord Jesus Christ, who hath blessed us with all spiritual blessings in the heavenly in Christ" (Eph. 1:3).

Such is the work which is now fully accomplished in and for the lowliest sinner who has believed on the Lord Jesus Christ. It is all superhuman and God alone could do it: nay, if man could even have any part in that work it would at that point of contact be imperfect, and therefore be blasted and ruined forever. These marvels of grace constitute that "good work" which He has but begun in those who trust Him. To this much more is yet to be added according to Phil. 1:6. "He that hath begun a good work in you, will perform it, until the day of Jesus Christ." The "riches of grace" are the beginning; the final presentation in glory in the likeness of Christ will be the completion. Such a final perfection and such an eternal being is the greatest divine undertaking for the one who has been lost in sin. Nothing less than this would satisfy the infinite love of God. That He might thus be free to satisfy His boundless love for us He met all the issues of sin for a lost and ruined world, and so perfectly has He wrought that man need now but believe and thus receive the bounty of His grace. It is "Grace reigning through righteousness." "For God has concluded them all in unbelief, that he might have mercy upon all. O the depth of the riches both of the wisdom and knowledge of God! How unsearchable are his judgments, and his ways past finding out! For who hath known the mind of the Lord? Or who hath been his counsellor? Or who hath first given to him, and it shall be recompensed unto him again? For of him, and through him, and to him, are all things: to whom be glory for ever. Amen."

CHAPTER VII

TWO CARDINAL FACTS

Of the foregoing thirty-three positions into which a believer is brought by the sufficient power and sovereign grace of God, two should be considered at length; both because of their prominence on the Sacred Pages and because of their fundamental character. They are both stated in John 14:20, and are the words of Christ: "Ye in me, and I in you." Though the choice of words here would remind one of the first page of a child's primer, these words, nevertheless, contain, in germ form, two great lines of truth which are subsequently developed in the Epistles of the New Testament. True these words present a paradox to human minds; but this may be but added evidence of their divine character. There are no paradoxes with God.

In this passage the saved one is first said to be "in Christ." This particular phrase, with its equivalent "in Him," is used many times in the New Testament and with deep meaning. It is found twenty-eight times in the first chapter of Ephesians alone. The phrase states a position in Christ which means nothing less than an organic union with Christ. This union is formed through the power of God when one is saved. It is the work of the Spirit by which a member is baptized into the one body. Two figures are used in the Bible to illustrate this union: The vine and the branches, and the head with its members in the body. We are familiar with the process of grafting a branch into a tree, but not so familiar with the thought of joining a member into a human body; yet this is the exact meaning of this Scripture. There is a time when the individual is without Christ; and again a time when, through believing, he is "in Christ." This stupendous change is described in 1 Cor. 12:13: "For by one Spirit are we all baptized into one body, whether we be Jews or Gentiles, whether we be bond or free; and have been all made to drink into one Spirit." This organism which is composed of Christ the Head and all the members joined to Him by the Spirit is that which in the Bible is called "the church which is his body." This must be distinguished from all outward, or visible, organizations. To this organism, His body, every believer is perfectly and eternally joined by the baptism of the Spirit at the instant he believes. He is then "in Christ."

To be in Christ is to possess a new standing before God; a standing which is no less than the infinite righteousness of God.

The word "righteousness" is used with four distinct meanings in the New Testament and the various meanings should always be held in mind. (1) God Himself is said to be righteous (Rom. 3:25, 26); (2) Self-righteousness, expressed by Paul as "mine own righteousness" (Phil. 3:9), "Their own righteousness" (Rom. 10:2); (3) A righteousness of daily life which is produced in the believer by the unhindered Spirit (Rom. 8:4); (4) The righteousness of God which is said to be reckoned to the one who believes: "A righteousness from God which is unto all and upon all who believe" (Rom. 3:22). The fourth meaning of the word is that aspect of righteousness which is now under consideration and that which provides the child of God with a perfect standing. This righteousness must be absolutely disassociated from all other forms of righteousness. It is not an attribute of God; it is in no way produced in life by the Spirit; and is as certainly unrelated to self-righteousness in every form. It is in no way related to right conduct. It is that which we become when we are vitally joined to Christ.

A human member severed from a body is both meritless and loathsome in itself; but if it were instantly and perfectly joined to a living body it would at once lose its former character, and from that time forth it would be recognized and honored as a part of the new body in which it is found. If that new organism was the body of the most honored person in the world, the new standing of that new member would be that of the one to whom it is joined. In like manner if that new person to whom a member is joined is the Christ of God, that new member will have a standing which is none other than the righteousness of God.

This, it must be repeated, is not a righteousness of man's making: it is distinctly said to be "made" unto the believer by God Himself. This is clear from the following passages: "Christ Jesus, who of God is made unto us * * * righteousness" (1 Cor. 1:30); "For he hath made him to be sin for us, who knew no sin; that we might be made the righteousness of God in him" (2 Cor. 5:21); "For I bear them record that they have a zeal of God, but not according to knowledge. For they being ignorant of God's righteousness, and going about to establish their own righteousness, have not submitted themselves unto the righteousness of God. For Christ is the end of the law for righteousness to every one that believeth" (Rom. 10:2-4); "That I may win Christ, and be found in him, not having mine own righteousness, which is of the law, but that which is through the faith of Christ, the righteousness which is of God by faith" (Phil. 3:8, 9); "But now the righteousness of God without the law is manifested, being witnessed by the law and the prophets; even the righteousness of God which is by faith of Jesus Christ unto all and upon all them that believe" (Rom. 3:21, 22); "For what saith the scriptures? Abraham believed God, and it was counted unto him for righteousness. Now to him that worketh is the reward not reckoned of grace, but of debt. But to him that worketh not, but believeth on him that justifieth the ungodly, his faith is counted for righteousness. Even as David also described the blessedness of the man, unto whom God imputeth righteousness without works" (Rom. 4:3-6); "And therefore it was imputed to him (Abraham) for righteousness. Now it was not written for his sake alone, that it was imputed unto him; but for us also, to whom it shall be imputed, if we believe on him that raised up Jesus our Lord from the dead; who was delivered for our offences, and was raised again for our justification" (Rom. 4:22-25); "Christ hath redeemed us from the curse of the law, being made a curse for us," and "He hath made us accepted in the beloved" (Gal. 3:13; Eph. 1:6); "I am not ashamed of the gospel of Christ, * * * For therein is the righteousness of God revealed (a righteousness from God) from faith to faith" (Rom. 1:16, 17).

Such are the marvels of His grace. Of ourselves we could be only conscious of our failure and sin, and wholly unable to provide a cure. He is able to make us the very righteousness of God in Christ. As we are made righteous in His sight, He is able to justify us now and forever "from all things from which we could not be justified by the law of Moses." "We are justified freely by his grace through the redemption which is in Christ Jesus."

This bestowed righteousness, then, is Christ who is the very righteousness of God, and He is made the righteousness of God unto us when we are found in Him. Such is the standing before God of every saved person whether he has come to understand his position or not.

There are practical values, however, in coming to know that we are now made the righteousness of God, and that this righteousness is so unrelated to our own merit, or demerit, and so related to Christ that it can and will abide without change through all eternity. Such knowledge will result in indescribable peace of soul. Oh the burden and yoke of a law that is always broken! The thought of a God Who is never satisfied! A standing that is always hopeless because of our utter helplessness! Then to know the liberty into which we have been brought that we need no longer vainly strive to make ourselves acceptable to God, but can believe that we are "made acceptable to God by Jesus Christ," and on no lower plain than that of the infinite Person of our Lord! There is indescribable rest and peace in realizing that we are already "accepted in the beloved." Such rest and peace would come to a multitude of God's children if they but knew and believed the word of His grace.

To know our perfect standing in Christ does not lead to laxity in daily life: it is the strongest possible incentive to holy living that human heart can know. Let there be no idle speculation here. It is the testimony of the Spirit of God we are dealing with, and that testimony is to the effect that man's merit, or demerit, cannot become a qualifying factor in the bestowed righteousness of God. It is distinctly for the one who "worketh not." Carelessness of life has never resulted from believing this revelation.

God is most evidently concerned with the quality of the daily life of His child; but such an issue cannot be raised here. The divine order cannot be safely ignored, which is first to reveal the grace position, and then to appeal for the corresponding manner of daily life. God's children are too often fed on mere injunctions with no reference to the corresponding and related positions. This will always result in a hardening of heart and carelessness of life. God has clearly related the position to the conduct and in a positive order, and it is perilous to omit any aspect of the truth or to change the divine order of its application. True heart-searching and moral judgments follow almost without exhortation in those who come to understand the exceeding grace of God in their behalf.

The second vital fact mentioned in John 14:20 is stated in the words of Christ, "I in you." Not only is the believer "in Christ," but Christ is in the believer. This is the fundamental Biblical fact concerning the Christian. He has received a deposit of eternal life, something entirely new to him, which is not known to any human being excepting those who have believed on Christ. Jesus said, "I am come that they might have life." This is a new life imparted, rather than a mere inspiration or example for living. It is on this sole point of possessing the new life that all Christian profession is to be judged. "Examine yourselves whether ye be in the faith; prove your own selves. Know ye not your own selves, how that Jesus Christ is in you, except ye be reprobates?" (2 Cor. 13:5). There are upwards of eighty-five New Testament passages referring directly to this fact of a new imparted divine life. When these are considered, it will be found that this life is never possessed by an unsaved person; but it is revealed to be as certainly the present possession of every saved person, even the least of all believers. "He that believeth on the Son hath everlasting life."

It is also revealed that this new life is none other than the indwelling Son of God. "He that hath the Son hath life; and he that hath not the Son of God hath not life" (1 John 5:12); "When Christ, who is our life, shall appear" (Col. 3:4); "Christ liveth in me" (Gal. 2:20); "Christ in you the hope of glory" (Col. 1:27). This indwelling One being the Son of God and eternal, the life is eternal. "I give unto them eternal life; and they shall never perish" (John 10:28); "The gift of God is eternal life through Jesus Christ our Lord" (Rom. 6:23).

This is the great supernatural fact of regeneration. By this regeneration legitimate children of God are formed who are by all right and title the true sons of God, and if sons, heirs of God and joint-heirs with Jesus Christ. They form a "new generation" or species, and their destiny is, in consonance with their new divine nature, in the eternal glory of the household and family of God.

The practical value of knowing this relation to God, or to be able to say, "Christ liveth in me," is but to be impelled to go on to the place wherein it may also be said, "and the life I now live, I live by the faith of the Son of God who loved me and gave himself for me." As certainly as a member is vitally joined to the body, so certainly the life of the Head flows into that member, and by this new vitality it is alive and in possession of every vital power. It also follows that such a member should be wholly submissive to the mind and will of the Head. How imperative, reasonable and blessed it is to be wholly yielded to Him that every thought of His great heart may find instant and perfect expression through every member in His own body!

CHAPTER VIII

ASSURANCE OF SALVATION

From the testimony of the Scriptures, a Christian should know that he is saved. There is abundant Biblical witness on this point, and it can hardly be deemed commendable to be in doubt on this vital question; yet to many it may seem to be presumptuous in the extreme for one to be assured of his own salvation. Where there is a lack of assurance there is usually an impression that so long as the daily life is quite imperfect (and how immodest it would be to claim that it is otherwise) it is unreasonable to do any more than hope that through some special exercise of mercy on God's part it will not be as bad in the end as it might otherwise be. Unwittingly such attitudes of mind disclose the appalling fact that persons who hold such views have never turned from dependence on their own works and merit to a dependence on the all-sufficient work and merit of Christ. If salvation depends in any degree on personal goodness, there could not be even a saved person in the world, and therefore no ground in it for assurance. Salvation is not offered to those who have purposed to be good, or religious, nor is it guaranteed to those who hope God will Himself be good and gracious in the end. It is offered to all meritless, helpless sinners who are willing to believe that God has already been good in that He has provided, in Christ, not only what they need now, but all they need in time and for eternity. This, too, is believed on no other evidence than that God has said it in His Word. In looking away from self and one's failure to Christ and His saving grace, one will find adequate grounds for a God-honoring certainty as to position and destiny in Christ Jesus. No life would ever be good enough to merit anything but condemnation from a holy God if judged on the grounds of moral equity. On the other hand, no sinner has fallen so low, or is so weak in himself, that he cannot find absolute rest and assurance of his salvation in looking away to Christ and the finished provisions of His grace. The attitude one may hold on the question of assurance may thus become somewhat of a test as to whether he has really believed on Christ, although it should not be assumed that such is invariably the case.

There are certain general facts about Christian assurance which may well be stated. The evidence underlying a positive conviction, or assurance as to personal salvation, is primarily the fact of the faithfulness of God as revealed in the Word. When God has made an unconditional declaration of His faithfulness, it is hardly becoming in one of His children to entertain any uncertainty in those things which He has promised. He has promised to save and keep all who put their trust in Him. Having put one's trust in Him for salvation, one must either believe Him to do what He has said, or in the measure in which one fails to do so suppose Him to be untrue.

At this point a doubt is sometimes expressed as to whether one has really believed in the saving way. As a matter of fact, such a doubt is still one in regard to himself rather than of God. This, of course, is another question altogether; but one so important that nothing else can be undertaken or determined until it is settled. The only cure for this uncertainty is to end it with certainty. Let such an one face his own utter sinfulness and meritlessness with the revelations of the cross and discover, as he must, no hope in himself, and then and there, once for all, appropriate the provisions of divine grace for every need of a sin-cursed soul. If need be, note the very day and hour of such a decision and then believe in the decision itself enough to thank God for His saving grace and faithfulness, and in every thought, act and word thereafter treat the decision as final and real. It is the crying need of a multitude of religious people that they bring themselves to some final dealing with the Son of God with regard to their sins and His salvation. They should be positive enough in this matter to face the eternal question before Him as to whether they choose to stand in His grace alone, or in something within themselves, even in the slightest degree. No very deep conviction of assurance can grow in any heart where the mind is still wondering whether it has really believed in a saving way, and where no impressions of certainty are allowed to take root. Confidence in the faithfulness of God will not thrive when one is constantly singing hymns which have been written to voice the position of the unsaved, such as the hymn in which one is assuming to be "coming to the cross." Let that issue be sealed and past, so far as salvation is concerned, and rather let one be occupied with those blessings which are vouchsafed to those who have believed. It would be much more reasonable to sing "In the cross of Christ I glory."

Assurance is born of confidence in Christ. He has said: "Him that cometh to me I will in no wise cast out." Having come, there is but one question remaining: "Has He cast me out?" This, it will be noted, is a serious question involving the very trust-worthiness of Christ. To doubt salvation at this point is not modest or commendable: it is the sin of distrusting God, or making Him untrue. Without faith it is impossible to please God. On the other hand, it is quite possible for one in facing this question to seal his confidence in God by a faithful "Amen" to every word God has spoken as to His plan and purpose in salvation. Who can look at the cross of Christ and not be convinced that God's love has been manifested toward us and that He Who paid such a price to redeem us will not instantly receive any soul that trusts in Him?

The word of Scripture becomes the title deed, or official writings, as to the certainty of the transaction. "These things have I written unto you that believe on the name of the Son of God; that ye may know that ye have eternal life." Such wonderful knowledge, therefore, is to be gained through the things written. The written things are His exceeding great and precious promises; but these promises can be of no avail to the heart that will not believe Him, or take Him at His word. Normal Christian experience and the joy and peace that results from believing can never even begin in the heart until God has been trusted to the extent that the record of His saving grace has been believed and received.

There is a normal Christian experience. There are new and blessed emotions and desires. Old things do pass away, and behold all things do become new; but all such experiences are but secondary evidence, as to the fact of salvation, in that they grow out of that positive repose of faith which is the primary evidence. There is very much Scripture about the results that are sure to appear in a transformed life. True salvation must result in just such realities. It is inconceivable that Christ should come to live in a human heart and its experiences remain unchanged. There must be, under such conditions, a new and vital relationship to God the Father, to fellow-Christians and to Christ Himself, a new attitude toward prayer, toward the Word, toward sin and toward the unsaved. This is the view-point of the Apostle James when he contends so earnestly for works that will justify. It must be remembered, however, that James is here concerned with the appearance our professions make to the outside world, rather than of our acceptance before God. Men can judge only by the outward appearance, and works alone can justify the Christian profession in their sight. God looks on the heart and before Him no works can avail. Before God man must be justified by faith alone. This, James clearly asserts to be true as illustrated in the case of Abraham (Jas. 2:23).

The First Epistle of John is full of references to the outward evidence of the inward fact of the newly imparted divine life. This little book, standing near the end of the Bible, may be taken, in one sense, as an examination of the believer. "Hereby we know that we know him, if we keep his commandments" (there is no reference here to the commandments of Moses); "In this the children of God are manifested, and the children of the devil: whoso doeth not righteousness is not of God (cf. John 6:28, 29), neither he that loveth not his brother"; "We know that we have passed from death unto life, because we love the brethren"; "Whosoever doeth not righteousness is not of God, neither he that loveth not his brother"; "And hereby we know that he abideth in us, by the Spirit which he hath given us"; "He that loveth not knoweth not God; for God is love"; "And we have seen and do testify that the Father sent the Son to be the Saviour of the world. Whosoever shall confess that Jesus is the Son of God, God dwelleth in him, and he in God" (cf. 1 Cor. 12:3).

Such a precious experience as is described by these passages may become clouded by sin or lost in the depression of some physical weakness, and were we depending upon the experience as primary evidence that we are saved, all grounds of assurance would be swept away. The primary evidence is clearly stated in the same Epistle as the final word of testing here given and the final grounds of confidence: "If we receive the witness of men, the witness of God is greater: for this is the witness of God which he hath testified of his Son. He that believeth on the Son of God hath the witness in himself: he that believeth not God hath made him a liar; because he believeth not the record that God gave of his Son. And this is the record, that God hath given to us eternal life, and this life is in his Son. He that hath the Son hath the life; and he that hath not the Son of God hath not the life. These things (about having the life) have I written unto you that believe on the name of the Son of God; that ye may know that ye have eternal life, and that ye may believe on the name of the Son of God" (1 John 5:9-13). The possession of the indwelling Son of God is the abiding fact of the newly created life in Him, and should never be confused with some imperfect and changeable experience in the daily life. He is received by faith. His presence most naturally leads to blessed new realities in experience. Certainly experience never leads to the realities of the presence of the indwelling Son of God.

The Bible use of the word "assurance" will be found in several passages: "Let us draw near with a true heart in full assurance of faith" (Heb. 10:22). This is the confidence that grows out of a repose of faith in the faithfulness of God that He will fulfill every word He has spoken. "And unto all riches of the full assurance of understanding" (Col. 2:2). This is the breadth of confidence that grows as one increasingly enters into the vastness of God's revelation of His grace in Christ Jesus. Some are so limited in spiritual vision when they believe that their first step in faith is centered on one promise alone. To such there will be a growing understanding and a corresponding increase of confidence and assurance as other promises and facts of grace are apprehended. "And we desire that every one of you do shew the same diligence of the full assurance of hope unto the end" (Heb. 6:11). Here is a reference to that assurance which is the full conviction that every promise and revelation concerning the future will be surely fulfilled. This, like all assurance, is simply the result of believing God.

CHAPTER IX

REWARDS, OR THE PLACE OF CHRISTIAN WORKS

True Christian living and service flow out of the new creation which is the result of the saving work of God and are divinely recognized by the promise of rewards. The Bible revelation concerning rewards not only presents a great incentive to holy and faithful living, but is a necessary counterpart of the doctrines of free grace. The divine plan of salvation under free grace is to save men "without money and without price." This means that no exchange is made. Man receives all that he has as a gift and only as a gift. It also means that there are no after payments to be made "on the installment plan," as though some attempted correctness of life and conduct could qualify the transaction of grace. What is done for man is done graciously. God will not suffer His gift to be confused with useless attempts to pay, or return, anything to Him in exchange. It is equally evident that it is not His purpose that Christian service shall be rendered as an attempt to return something for what He has done, notwithstanding the fact that such motives in service are sometimes urged by the misinformed.

God is said to be actuated by at least three motives in saving men: First, they are said to be "created in Christ

Jesus unto good works, which God hath before ordained that they should walk in them." This, it is evident, is the least of all. It is, however, the only motive that is sometimes presented. "We are saved to serve" is a common phrase which if taken alone would represent the Father as seeking our service only and as debased to the level of the most sordid commercialist. It is true rather that we are saved in order that we may serve. There can be no true service apart from salvation. Service then becomes a divinely provided privilege. Second, we are saved that "we might not perish, but have everlasting life." This would seem of greatest importance, for it represents our unmeasured and eternal blessing in Him. But there is a third divine motive infinitely beyond these which, we may believe, is the highest motive of saving grace: namely, we are saved "that in the ages to come he might shew the exceeding riches of his grace in his kindness toward us through Christ Jesus." The result of that kindness toward us will be seen to be the final form in which we appear in the glory when we are "conformed to the image of his Son." Every being in the universe will know what we were and will behold the spectacle of what we are in that final and eternal glory. This transformation will have measured the grace of God for us, and on that scale which will be wholly satisfying to Himself. He will have made a demonstration of His grace before all created beings which will be to His own exceeding joy.

It may be concluded, then, that God is moved to act in our behalf from the sole motive of love toward us and not for gains of any kind whatsoever. It is all to unfold His grace alone. Thus the new-born child in the Father's house begins his career with no hopeless debt. He has simply to enter into that which is his by all right and title in the amazing grace of God. When the Christian enters into service the greatest care must be exercised that the very motives for service do not in some way violate these most precious relations of divine favor. It will not do to attempt to repay Him by service for what He has done. A gift is not appreciated as such by the recipient when there is the slightest intention even to pay for it. Yet the stupid human heart is so often proposing to repay God for His mercy. Such words are put into the lips of Christ in the hymn, "I gave my life for thee, what hast thou given for me?" The question "what hast thou given for me?" may well be asked of us all; but never as though it was a "dun" for a long unpaid debt to Him.

The only true motive for Christian life and service is the very one motive which has actuated God in His service for us. It is just LOVE. Salvation was to reveal and satisfy His love for us. "God commendeth his love toward us, in that, while we were yet sinners, Christ died for us" (Rom. 5:8). "Hereby perceive we the love of God, because he laid down his life for us" (1 John 3:16). It then follows that "we ought to lay down our lives for the brethren"; but never to pay Him for laying down His life for us. It is rather that we act on the same principle of love. We can make no claim on Him whatsoever. At best, from our own standpoint, we are "unprofitable servants." He will reward every faithful service; but He will not demand the service. His recognition of Christian service will be but another manifestation of His marvelous grace. No child of God is "earning his way." Such a thought might satisfy a sordid commercial

instinct of an untaught heart, but the thought is foreign to a normal relation of the child to his Father. "He hath given us all things richly to enjoy." The Father's supply of our temporal needs may come through the very channel in which our service is rendered, but it must not be deemed a payment for that service or all truth is subverted. His care for us is in pure love which can be claimed by the most helpless invalid as much as by the most active person. He does not promise to care for us if we "deliver the tale of bricks." Such doctrine belongs to the Egyptian taskmasters of old. God is just as much committed to care for us, by His loving promises, after our vitality is exhausted as when we are in the prime of life and strength. "They that serve in the gospel shall live by the gospel" is a divine exhortation to those who have the privilege of love gifts to the gospel ministry. It is not addressed to the minister. "Give and it shall be given to you" is an assurance that you cannot approach the Father with an expression of your love to Him that He will not meet you with a vastly greater response of His overflowing grace. "Seek ye first the kingdom of God, and his righteousness; and all these things shall be added unto you" is not an injunction to seek an increase in salary, even as a secondary consideration. It is forgetting all else but Him, and the divine response is to the end that "All these (temporal) things shall be added unto you."

Every service for God, then, should be, like His, a service expressing love, and all occupation in life should be deemed by the Christian as a service for God (1 Cor. 10:31; Eph. 6:6-8; Col. 3:22-24). God does not need our paltry gifts: He wants us. He is not looking for free labor from us: He is looking for evidence of our love for Him. Service for a salary is a poor return: service for His own sake is most precious in His eyes. There is no commercialism in the household of God, for there the standard of value is only love. "He brought me to the banqueting house, and his banner over me was love." "She hath loved much" was a priceless verdict of Christ. For such service of love there will be a divine recognition in the coming glory. This will be shown by the bestowal of rewards.

It should also be stated that Christian service is not any good act we may choose to perform. The child of God has been "created in Christ Jesus unto good works, which God hath before ordained that we should walk in them." This means that there is a design and field of service divinely planned for each one, and "good works" in the Bible sense can only be the finding and doing of that which He has ordained. The works are "good" in that they are "that good, and acceptable, and perfect, will of God" for each believer. These can only be entered into by His divine direction, which will be realized by all who wholly yield to Him. Service must be "where he will."

God has promised by many Scriptures to recognize all service that is rendered as a love-expression to Him and all that is within the gracious plan of life He has made for every child of His. There will be rewards, crowns and prizes. No one can define them. They most evidently speak of His loving appreciation of our little suffering and faithfulness for Him. They will be inexpressibly sweet, and they will abide for all eternity. Salvation is not a reward for the believer's service. Salvation is God's work for us. Rewards are always connected with the believer's works and merit. The rewards are to be bestowed at "the judgment-seat of Christ" (2 Cor. 5:10). This is when the saints are gathered to meet their Lord in the air (1 Cor. 4:5; 2 Tim. 4:8; Rev. 22:12; Mt. 16:27; Lk. 14:14). It will be a moment of discovery as to who hath loved much and who was much occupied with Him. It is most comforting to read of that very time of judgment, "and then shall every man have praise of God" (1 Cor. 4:5).

Of the many passages in the Bible on rewards, two

may be considered here. The first, 1 Cor. 9:18-27, is the divinely recorded illustration of true service as seen in the life of the Apostle Paul. This passage opens with the question: "What is my reward then?" This is followed by a description of the tireless service and faithfulness of the Apostle. At the twenty-fifth verse he presents an illustration based on the Grecian games. "Know ye not that they which run in a race run all, but one receiveth the prize? So run, that ye may obtain." The most violent effort of the runner in the race is, in the illustration, the standard of effort for the servant of God. "And every man that striveth for the mastery is temperate in all things." There is the greatest care of the body that it may be found at its highest state of efficiency in agility, strength and endurance.. "Now they (the athletes) do it (sacrifice their desires and every indulgence and carefully train) to obtain a corruptible crown." What was more transitory than the wreath of leaves that was placed on the victor's brow? "But we (sacrifice our desires and indulgences and train ourselves for) an incorruptible crown." If only such were true! Few have so lived before God as did the Apostle Paul. How shame must cover us when we think of the ceaseless effort of the worldly athlete to gain a fading crown that soon will be forever forgotten, while God is offering to us an incorruptible crown the effulgence of which will be increasing in brightness when all the contests of earth are forgotten in the ages of the ages! This passage closes with a personal testimony from the Apostle. "I therefore so run, not as uncertainly; so fight I, not as one that beateth the air: but I keep under my body, and bring it into subjection: lest that by any means when I have preached to others, I myself should be a castaway" (disapproved). There is no reference to salvation in this passage. It begins with the words: "What is my reward then?" and is of rewards throughout. The fear that is expressed at the end is of being disapproved of the Lord. It is not fear of being found unsaved. This would be opposed to the unvarying and always consistent teaching of the Apostle concerning the grounds of salvation. He testifies that there is a half-hearted preaching which would disappoint His Lord. He is striving that he may be approved as a faithful servant in that ministry to which he was called.

The second Scripture to be mentioned on rewards is 1 Cor. 3:9-15. This presents the fact of rewards as certainly promised by God. "For we are labourers together with God: ye are God's husbandry, ye are God's building. According to the grace of God which is given unto me, as a wise master builder, I have laid the foundation, and another buildeth thereon. But let every man take heed how he buildeth thereupon. For other foundation can no man lay than that is laid, which is Jesus Christ." This is not the building of character, which undertaking is unknown in the Scriptures. It is rather the building of service unto a reward. Christ is the foundation and to be on Him is to be saved. It is possible to build on Him of very different spiritual substances, but all built on the same foundation, Christ. Such are the possibilities in service for all who are saved in Christ. "Now if any man build upon this foundation gold, silver, precious stones, wood, hay, stubble; every man's work (not his salvation) shall be made manifest: for the day shall declare it, because it shall be revealed by fire; and the fire shall try every man's work of what sort it is. If any man's work abide which he hath built there upon (Christ), he shall receive a reward. If any man's work (built on Christ the Foundation) shall be burned, he shall suffer loss: but he himself shall be saved; yet so as by fire."

Fire is the symbol of the judgment by which the superstructure of Christian works is to be tested. Jesus made use of another symbol of judgment, the floods of water, that shall test the foundation. Woe to those who are found building on the sand! Not only will their superstructure of self-righteousness collapse, but their foundation, the fallen nature, will be swept by the waters of judgment into everlasting darkness. Although secure against the floods, established on the Rock Christ Jesus, great sorrow and shame will come upon those saved ones who have had all the days of grace and the enabling power of God and a field so white for harvest and in the end present a completed service of "wood, hay, stubble" only.

Thus it may be concluded that we are saved in the boundless grace of God and His attitude toward us is ever and always one of love. We are the objects of His bounty and care. Being saved, we are privileged to enter some service of His eternal design. This is not a field in which to compensate Him for His love. It is our divinely given opportunity to express our love to Him to the praise of the Glory of His grace. He recognizes such ministries of love by that which He has been pleased to call "rewards." What more could He do than He has done? How more faithfully could He appeal for our heart's devotion to Him?

CHAPTER X

THE ETERNAL SECURITY OF THE BELIEVER

The So-called "Doubtful Passages" Part I

The question here raised and which has been so long under theological controversy is simply stated in the words, "Can a person once saved be lost again?" To this question two widely differing answers have been given, which are as simply stated in the two words, Yes and No. There is no middle position, or ground for compromise, for both answers cannot be true at the same time. One cannot really be secure if he is insecure as to his eternal keeping by the slightest degree.

The subject of security is somewhat different from the question of assurance already considered. Eternal security is a doctrine of Scripture, a divine revelation of an abiding fact which exists, whether it is believed or not. Assurance is only the personal confidence in a present salvation.

The two schools of belief regarding eternal security have existed for several centuries and certain church creeds have taken positive sides on the question. The belief, or disbelief, in security is, however, more of a personal matter than credal; depending much on the extent of personal Bible study and heart response to the whole revelation of God. Because one is enrolled under a

"Calvinistic" creed does not guarantee that he will himself be free from the distractions of mere human reason: on the other hand, because one is enrolled under an "Arminian" creed is no guaranty that he will not eventually learn to rest in every revelation and promise of God.

The question resolves itself to one issue: did Christ do enough on the cross to make it possible for God righteously to keep one saved, as well as righteously to save at all? Since this question strikes at the very heart of the revelation regarding the cross, its importance cannot be overestimated. The solution of the question involves the very foundation of personal rest and peace, and must qualify Christian service as well. No one can rest while in terror of eternal damnation, nor can one be normal in service if he is confronted with the superhuman task of self-keeping in the realm of the new creation.

A careful survey of the whole field of discussion regarding the security of those who are saved will reveal that one group return constantly in their discussions of this subject to the conclusions of human reason, to the uncertain evidence of human experience, and such Scripture as is cited by them, they "wrest to their own destruction." The other group are guided by revelation alone, believing that there is nothing about any phase of salvation that can be explained within the circumscribed limits of unaided reason or knowledge. Salvation began with God in another sphere, and its conditions, character and results are altogether in harmony with the eternal being of God, rather than with the vain imaginations of fallen man. Not one step can be taken toward salvation until the individual is prepared to project his confidence beyond the sphere of human understanding, and believe something of the unseen and otherwise unknowable as it is disclosed in the Word of God. This discussion is undertaken with the hope that it may enable some who have hesitated to go all the way in faith to be more able to do so to the glory of our covenant-keeping God. It need hardly be added that this discussion has only to do with the security of those who are saved in the true and Biblical sense. There is no divine promise of keeping for the mere professor who does not truly believe.

There are a few passages which have been thought by some to teach that salvation is insecure. These are to be taken up first. Following the consideration of these the more positive teachings of the Scriptures will be presented.

In taking up these so-called "insecurity passages," which number about twenty-five, it will be found that they have been given the character of doubt as to the keeping power of God only through misinterpretation. Thus they are made to contradict the much larger body of Scripture in which an absolute security is promised. The misinterpretation will usually be easily discovered by a careful examination of the whole context. Some of the passages to be taken up, it may be stated, have always been considered difficult, this being evidenced by the various renderings and expositions. It should not be concluded, however, that teaching of insecurity is warranted from the difficulties in these passages. The various renderings and expositions made by creditable expositors do not present teachings foreign to the whole counsel of God. God forbid that any effort should be made to "harmonize the Word of God." It is a consistent whole in its testimony, and only awaits our right understanding of all that it teaches. It will not do, therefore, to discredit the clear testimony of a "verily" of the Scriptures with an "if."

The passages in question may best be treated under classified groupings, and for want of space consideration of every passage will not be undertaken. What is true of one passage within a group will be found in the main to be true of the others.

I. Passages Dispensationally Misapplied.

Mt. 24:13 (see also Mk. 13:13; Mt. 10:22): "But he that shall endure unto the end, the same shall be saved." This passage occurs in the midst of the "Olivet discourse," which was addressed to Israel only. They alone are "hated of all nations" (vs. 9). The context is a description of "sorrow" and "the great tribulation" (vs. 8 and 21), which period cannot even begin on the earth until the Church has been removed (1 Thess. 5:9; 4:13-18). It cannot, and does not, apply to any saint of this dispensation. There is a sweet promise here for those in that terrible time who endure to its end.

Ezk. 33:7, 8 was true under the law; but is not true under grace.

Mt. 18:23-35 (cf. Mt. 25:30; 20:1-16) is of "servants" in God's vineyard, Israel. This is to be distinguished from the present preaching of the gospel in the "field" which is the world. Forgiveness under the law was as ye forgive (Mt. 6:14, 15). Forgiveness under grace is, like all gifts of grace, first, divinely bestowed, and then becomes an incentive in the believer's heart to exercise the same toward others (Eph. 4:32). It must be noted that "servants" are not necessarily saved.

II. The False Teachers of "the Last Days."

1 Tim. 4:1, 2: "Now the Spirit speaketh expressly, that

in the latter times some shall depart from the faith, giving
heed to seducing spirits, and doctrines of devils; speaking
lies in hypocrisy; having their conscience seared with a
hot iron." There is no reference here to personal faith.
Those mentioned are said to depart from the faith. This is
"the faith which was once delivered to the saints" (Jude
3). Very much of 2 Thess., 2 Tim., 2 Pet., 2 John, 3 John
and Jude concerns the "last days" just before the Church is
removed from the earth. None of the New Testament
Epistles are concerned with the Great Tribulation which
follows the taking away of the Church; for the Tribulation
has to do with Israel and the Nations. The Church is
warned by an overwhelming body of Scripture against a
coming apostasy and that false teaching which is to
characterize her "last days" upon the earth. The false
teacher who has turned from the Truth is never said to be
saved; but God's judgment of him is sure. The above-
named Epistles should all be studied with this in mind,
especially 2 Tim. 3:1-5; 4:3, 4; 2 Pet. 2:1-22; 3:3, 4; 2
John 9-11, and Jude 4-19. Jude writes of these false
teachers as "they who separate themselves, sensual,
having not the Spirit."

III. Moral Reformation.

Lk. 11:24-26: "When the unclean spirit is gone out of a
man, he walketh through dry places, seeking rest; and
finding none, he saith, I will return unto my house whence
I came out. And when he cometh, he findeth it swept and
garnished. Then goeth he, and taketh to him seven other
spirits more wicked than himself; and they enter in, and
dwell there: and the last state of that man is worse than the
first." The Lord's object in thus presenting this truth was
evidently to set forth the futility of mere moral
reformation. Such a situation could never describe a

Christian who from the moment he is saved is indwelt by the Spirit and by Christ.

IV. Christian Profession is Proven by Its Fruits.

1 John 3:10: "In this the children of God are manifested, and the children of the devil: whosoever doeth not righteousness is not of God (note the fundamental divine requirement as stated in John 6:28, 29), neither he that loveth not his brother." There is an important distinction to be made between enduring in order to be saved and enduring because one is saved. The Bible consistently presents the latter test. "If ye continue in my words, then are ye my disciples indeed" (John 8:31). Of all the seed sown in the field but a small fraction became "wheat," the children of the kingdom. The rest sprang up, and was withered, or was caught away, or was choked. The present age is characterized by much merely formal profession. Within the mass of professors is the true "wheat." The divine test is always with regard to the essential character of the true child of God. As compared with the impotent, unregenerate nature, the divine nature does not sin, but tends to new aspirations and characteristics in daily life. It is so, and it must be so. The child of God still has the flesh, and this is said, to "lust against the Spirit." The new nature does not commit sin: the old nature can do nothing else. Proof that one is saved is not found in sinless perfection; but is found in the fact that there are new desires and powers in the new creation. These can prevail over the old desires by the power of the Spirit. The Bible simply demands that there shall be some real evidence of the new life from God.

2 Pet. 1:10: "Wherefore the rather, brethren, give diligence to make your calling and election sure: for if ye do these things (mentioned in vs. 6-8) ye shall never fall"

(stumble). Election is certainly of God (Rom. 8:29). Peter, here, calls on the saints to make full proof, or to give real evidence of their election by the presence of certain virtues in their lives which he has just mentioned in the preceding verses. So, also, Rom. 8:16-18 states that true children of God will suffer with Christ, rather than that they become children, or remain children by suffering. Rom. 8:13: "For if ye live after the flesh, ye shall die" (ye are on the way to die) is qualified by verse nine: "But ye are not in the flesh, but in the Spirit, if so be that the Spirit of God dwell in you. Now if any man have not the Spirit of Christ, he is none of his." It is this chapter of this great Epistle of salvation, it should be remembered, which presents the most unqualified revelations of security for the one who believes.

John 15:6: "If a man abide not in me, he is cast forth as a branch, and is withered; and men gather them, and cast them into the fire, and they are burned." This difficult passage may best be understood in its probable relation to professors. The reference is to "a man" and not to a branch, as in verse two. In such a case "abide not in me" could hardly mean more than a pretense, or false profession which "men" disallow as they would gather and burn dead branches. This, like James 2:14-26, is a matter of justification before men by works which testify to the fact of the presence or absence of the new life. Men are judged only by the outward: "God looketh on the heart," and "He knoweth them that are his." The whole Epistle of 1 John is filled with these practical tests of the Christian's life and conduct. To this may be added 1 Cor. 15:1, 2 and Heb. 3:6, 14.

V. Various Warnings.

1. Christians are warned: Rom. 14:15, "Destroy not

him with thy meat, for whom Christ died." The effect of this sin is defined in 1 Cor. 8:11, 12: "But when ye sin so against the brethren, and wound their weak conscience, ye sin against Christ." The effect of such sin is, therefore, the wounding of the weak conscience. The sin is most serious; but a true child of God will "never perish," and "will never die" (John 10:28; 11:26).

2. Professors are warned: Mt. 25:1-13 is of the ten virgins. Five had no oil, the symbol of divine life, though they had every outward appearance. They heard the judgment "I know you not," which could not be said of the least child of God.

3. Jews are warned: Heb. 10:26, "If we sin wilfully after we have received the knowledge of the truth, there remaineth no more a sacrifice for sins." The old Jewish sacrifices had passed and there was no longer that cure for sins. It was either to take Christ, who had died the sacrificial death for all, or to come into terrible judgment.

Heb. 6:4-9, "For it is impossible for those who were once enlightened, and have tasted of the heavenly gift, and were made partakers of the Holy Ghost, and have tasted of the good word of God, and the powers of the world to come, if they shall fall away, to renew them again unto repentance; seeing they crucify to themselves the Son of God afresh, and put him to an open shame." "But, beloved, we are persuaded better things of you, and things that accompany salvation, though we thus speak" (vs. 9). Much is said here as having been divinely accomplished in certain individuals, but it is not a sufficient description of the true child of God; who is light; who is already a citizen of heaven; who has been sealed by the Holy Spirit; who has been regenerated by the washing of the Word; and who has been recreated by the power of God. The passage is addressed to Hebrews and the first part of the chapter concerns their duty of passing from the elements of Jewish faith to Christ, and the warning is of their particular danger of substituting half truths for the full truth in Christ. That the passage is not for Christians is most evident from the closing verse of the context (vs. 9), which is preceded by the illustration found in verses seven and eight.

4. Gentiles are warned: Rom. 11:21, "For if God spared not the natural branches, take heed lest he also spare not thee." This message is addressed to Gentiles as contrasted to Israel, and is a distinction between God's dealing with Israel in one dispensation and with the mass of Gentiles in another dispensation, rather than a warning to saved individuals.

5. Two general warnings: Rev. 22:19, "And if any man shall take away from the words of the book of this prophecy, God shall take away his part out of the book of life, and out of the holy city, and from the things that are written in this book." The warning is most general. That no child of God would be permitted to do this, or to come under this judgment, is assured in 1 Cor. 10:13 and John 10:29.

1 Cor. 3:17, "If any man defile the temple of God, him shall God destroy (corrupt); for the temple of God is holy, which temple ye are." Another general warning of judgments which could never be the fate of the child of the Father (John 17:11).

VI. Christians May Lose Their Rewards, Walk in the Dark, or be Chastened.

1. Rewards may be forfeited, or lost, but this cannot be

said of salvation. 1 Cor. 9:27: "But I keep under my body, and bring it into subjection: lest that by any means, when I have preached to others, I myself should be a castaway" (disapproved). The context is only of rewards and not at all of salvation. The word here translated "castaway" is _adokimos, which is the negative form, by the prefix _a, of _dokimos. The negative form is translated by three English words in the New Testament: "castaway," once; "rejected," once; and "reprobate," six times. Three of the translations of "reprobate" are given a marginal rendering "void of judgment." Four meanings given to the word by the lexicons are "unable to stand test," "rejected," "refuse" and "worthless." The less severe form of the word is by the lexicons given first, which corresponds with the meaning given to it in the numerous translations in the Bible. The moderate meaning of the negative form of this word is demanded in the passage in question for at least four reasons. (1) The affirmative form of the word _dokimos, used in the New Testament six times, is always translated in the Bible and defined by the lexicographers, as well, as meaning "approved," or "to stand test." "For he that in these things serveth Christ is acceptable to God, and approved of men" (Rom. 14:18); "Salute Apelles approved in Christ" (Rom. 16:10); "For there must be also heresies among you, that they which are approved may be made manifest among you" (1 Cor. 11:19); "For not he that commendeth himself is approved, but whom the Lord commendeth" (2 Cor. 10:18); "Study to show thyself approved unto God, a workman that needeth not to be ashamed, rightly dividing the word of truth" (2 Tim. 2:15); "Blessed is the man that endureth temptation: for when he is tried, he shall receive the crown of life which the Lord hath promised to them that love him" (Jas. 1:12). If _dokimos is always "approved," or "tested" as to rewards, it follows that its negative form is naturally "disapproved" or "failure under testing." (2) To give _adokimos the severest possible meaning of being "cast off forever" would be to ignore wholly the meaning in the context. This is of rewards to the believer for faithful service. The passage opens with the words (vs. 18) "What then is my reward?" And Paul's fear, as has been before stated, is lest through half-hearted ministry he should be disapproved. Salvation is not in question, for salvation is not once related in the Scriptures to _dokimos, the affirmative form of this word. (3) To give _adokimos the severest meaning in this passage would be to bring it into direct opposition to all the great promises of God concerning His purpose and power in salvation. (4) It is to choose a meaning of the word which is remote and in no way the usual use made of it in the Scriptures. Conybeare and Howson render the passage: "But I bruise my body and force it into bondage; lest, perchance, having called others to the contest, I should myself fail shamefully of the prize" (Life of St. Paul, Chapter 12).

1 Cor. 3:15. "If any (Christians) man's work shall be burned, he shall suffer loss: but he himself shall be saved; yet so as by fire." The whole context, again, is of rewards for Christian service. The work of God must stand. The child of God will himself be saved, though all his works are burned.

Col. 1:21-23. "And you, that were sometimes alienated and enemies in your minds by wicked works, yet now hath he reconciled in the body of his flesh through death" (this is the work of God in salvation), "to present you holy and unblameable and unreprovable in his sight" (depends, not on His salvation, but); "if ye continue in the faith grounded and settled, and be not moved away from the hope of the gospel, which ye have heard."

2. Christian fellowship may be lost through sin: "If we say that we have fellowship with him, and walk in darkness, we lie, and do not the truth" (1 John 1:6). This passage has to do with loss of fellowship (not salvation) through sin. The cure for a Christian's sin is not in a second regeneration and justification by faith, but rather, "If we confess our sins, he is faithful and just to forgive us our sins, and to cleanse us from all unrighteousness" (vs. 9). This is the believer's way back into blessed joy and fellowship with his Lord, and should never be confused with the establishment of the eternal grounds of salvation. The unregenerate are not saved by confessing, but by believing. Thus the Prodigal Son, representing the possible return of the Jewish publicans and sinners under the Jewish covenants and relationships, returned to his father on the ground of confession, and not by a birth, or generation. He was lost and was found, which has not the same significance as being lost and saved. He never ceased to be a son, and was restored to the former relation to his father by confession: "Father, I have sinned against heaven and in thy sight, and am no more worthy to be called thy son." The same underlying truth will be found in the other parts of the same parable: "The lost sheep" and "The lost coin." Thus a saint of this dispensation, being under the new covenant, may return to his place of blessing by confession (1 John 1:9). David did not pray that his salvation might be restored after his great sin; but he did pray: "Restore unto me the joys of my salvation," and that after his full confession had been made.

3. Christians may be chastened: 1 Cor. 11:29-32. "For he that eateth and drinketh unworthily, eateth and drinketh damnation (judgment) unto himself, not discerning the Lord's body. For this cause many are weak and sickly among you, and many sleep. For if we would judge

ourselves, we would not be judged. But when we are judged, we are chastened of the Lord that we should not be condemned with the world." This passage has to do with a possible eating and drinking at the Lord's table in an unworthy manner, and the table is referred to in this passage as being an outward evidence of the believer's true fellowship with his Lord. He is thus warned against going to that table when there is unconfessed sin in his life, by that act assuming to be in fellowship with his Lord when he is not. The Father's method of dealing with His sinning child is then revealed. The sinning child may first judge himself, which he does by confessing his sins. If he judge not himself, he must be judged of his Father; but the Father's judgment is always chastisement and never condemnation with the world. The chastisement for the unyielding child, according to this passage, is that he may become "weak," "sick," or "sleep" (physical death).

John 15:2. "Every branch in me that beareth not fruit he taketh away." The reference is evidently to true branches, which is not the case in verse six. From the fact that the Greek word _airo has the meaning "lifting up out of its place," here translated from _airei, "taketh away," it would seem probable that the reference is to the last form of chastisement mentioned in 1 Cor. 11:30. Such branches are taken home to be with the Lord (see, also, 1 Tim. 5:12, "Having judgment" which is chastisement for a child of God).

VII. Christians May Fall From Grace.

Gal. 5:1-4. "Stand fast therefore in the liberty wherewith Christ hath set us free, and be not entangled again with the yoke of bondage. Behold, I Paul say unto you, that if ye be circumcised, Christ shall profit you nothing. For I testify again to every man that is circumcised, that he is a debtor to do the whole law. Christ is become of no effect unto you, whosoever of you are justified by the law; ye are fallen from grace." "Falling from grace," it will be seen from this passage, is not caused by sinning. It is simply departing from the liberty wherewith Christ hath set us free. It is returning to the yoke and bondage of the law from which the death of Christ hath delivered us. Returning to the law, the liberty which is ours in Christ is lost, and Christ, as the grounds of liberty, is of no effect. It is all a question of the enjoyment of that priceless liberty in grace. There is not the slightest hint in the passage that God withdraws His grace, or that any aspect of salvation has been canceled. It is probable that many believers have never had a vision of their liberty in Christ; but this passage is of those who have known such liberty and then have been drawn back into the yoke and bondage of law observance.

From the foregoing it may be concluded that there is no Scripture, when rightly divided and related to the whole testimony of God, that teaches that a Christian may be lost. Nor is there any such example in the Bible. Of all the incidents and parables, none can be made to teach the loss of salvation. Moreover, if it were possible to lose it, there is no promise, or hint, in the Bible that it could be regained. The Bible reveals nothing concerning repetition of regeneration.

There are at least five general and common questions of doubt that are often raised which should also be considered before turning to the positive revelation regarding eternal security.

1. What if a believer's faith should fail?

Faith, it may be answered, is not meritorious. We are

not saved because we possess the saving virtue of faith. We are saved through faith, and because of the grace of God. Incidentally faith is the only possible response of the heart to that grace. Saving faith is an act: not an attitude. Its work is accomplished when its object has been gained.

2. What if a Christian dies with unconfessed sin?

It is quite impossible that any believer knows, remembers, or has confessed every sin. Confession, after all, is but telling Him, and this could better be done, perhaps, in His gracious presence than otherwise. It is impossible that any would see His face if whole confession, or sinless perfection, should be made the condition of entering that blessed Presence. This question grows out of a very imperfect understanding of the finished work of Christ. Christ has died that sin might not keep us from God.

3. Does not the doctrine of security license people to sin?

Biblically, No; Experimentally, No. There is no greater incentive to holiness of life than to know one's own eternal position in Christ Jesus. It is, according to the Bible, God's superlative appeal for true Christian living. To the question, "Shall we continue in sin that grace may abound?" the unregenerate would answer "yes"; for that would be the voice of the fallen nature: but the regenerate will answer, "God forbid." To claim that teaching the doctrine of security will license people to sin is to ignore the mighty revelations of the believer's positions and the effect of these upon the life. It is to ignore the fact of the new divine nature which indwells each child of God. It is to ignore the new dispositions and tendencies flowing out of that new life. It is to ignore the imparted energy of God, "for it is God which worketh in you both to will and to do of his good pleasure." It is to challenge every revelation concerning God's plan of dealing with His child.

Experimentally no truly born-again persons have been known to live on a lower plane after they were saved than the plane on which they lived before they were saved, and very few have been known to take advantage of grace. Mere conversion, or reformation, may result in a return to a worse estate (Lk. 11:24-26). On the other hand, to hold over people the superhuman obligation of self-keeping in Christ, is but to discourage them utterly in the purpose of true Christian living and incline them to discount the very standards of God. Such must ever be called from a back-slidden state. The Puritans were not self-named. The name was given them because of their great carefulness of life and piety. Yet every Puritan believed in security, and they may be classed with a multitude of the most devoted saints who have lived and believed according to the testimony of God.

4. Cannot we rebel and be released from Christ if we so choose?

A most unscriptural emphasis upon the supposed power of the human will has been made by some. The human will never acts alone (saved persons, Phil. 2:13; unsaved persons, Eph. 2:2), and God has undertaken to keep His own from all such sin. "And the Lord shall deliver me from every evil work, and will preserve me unto his heavenly kingdom" (2 Tim. 4:18); "There hath no temptation taken you but such as is common to man: but God is faithful, who will not suffer you to be tempted above that ye are able; but will with the temptation also make a way to escape, that ye may be able to bear it" (1 Cor. 10:13); "I give unto them eternal life; and they shall never perish" (John 10:28); "Who are kept by the power of God through faith unto salvation ready to be revealed in the last time" (1 Pet. 1:5). Having really tasted the riches of His infinite grace and then preferring to be lost again would be the clearest evidence of insanity. We may be assured that God keeps any child of His who is so unfortunate as to lose his reason, and if such an one were to ask to be unsaved, and if it were possible, that one would be kept by the power of God through the dark night of insanity. For this he would give unceasing thanks to the Father through the ages to come.

5. Why the failure of so many converts?

No one can really judge another; but it is evident that converts who fail are either misguided professors "who went out from us because they were not of us" (1 John 2:19), or they are saved and perhaps so poorly taught, or so neglected in shepherd care, that they are utterly confused and are "walking in darkness" (1 John 1:6).

Conversion is but a human act of turning about. It can be done many times and even a believer may be converted (Lk. 22:32). Being born again is a different experience entirely. With it there is no repetition whatever, nor occasion for repetition. Some modern revival converts who have heard nothing but appeals for reformation and a general exhortation to be identified with religion, can hardly be expected to come under the same gracious keeping of God, as the one who has come to God by Jesus Christ, and who has intelligently rested in the saving grace of God as revealed in His Son.

CHAPTER XI

THE ETERNAL SECURITY OF THE BELIEVER

The Doctrine of the Scriptures Part II

The eternal security of the believer is revealed in a well-defined body of Scripture the interpretation of which is not subject to question as to its exact meaning, or as to the fact that it refers only to salvation, if the plain teaching of the Word of God is taken to be the final statement of truth. Those passages which have been thought by some to teach that a Christian might be lost again, together with certain questions of doubt, have been considered in the preceding chapter, and the way is clear, so far as this discussion is concerned, to give undivided attention to the positive words of certainty regarding the divine keeping guaranteed in the Word to every child of God. Complete exposition of this extensive body of Scripture would be impossible within the limits of this chapter. As in the preceding chapter, the passages may best be grouped under certain general heads, and representative passages of the Scriptures in this body of truth considered in each of these divisions. According to His Word, the true child of God is secure in the divine keeping for at least seven reasons:

I. The Purpose, Power and Present Attitude of God the Father.

1. The Purpose of God.

The divine revelation unfolds the eternal past, the present order in time, and the eternal future. To all these the saved one is closely related. From the beginning he was in the thought and purpose of God; he is now in the day of decision and grace; and the eternity to come is made glorious by the sure realization of the design of God for him. "For whom he did foreknow, he also did predestinate to be conformed to the image of his Son, that he might be the firstborn among many brethren, moreover whom he did predestinate, them he also called: and whom he called, them he also justified: and whom he justified, them he also glorified" (Rom. 8:29, 30). "According as he hath chosen us in him before the foundation of the world, that we should be holy and without blame before him" (Eph. 1:4).

These passages sweep the whole eternity. They reveal a divine purpose in the dateless past and reach on to its realization in the eternity to come, and all without reference to human conditions. Still another passage, related only to the ages to come, reveals that this will all be accomplished as a sufficient display, to all created beings, of the grace of God: "And hath raised us up together, and made us sit together in the heavenly in Christ Jesus: that in the ages to come he might show the exceeding riches of his grace in his kindness toward us through Christ Jesus" (Eph. 2:6, 7).

The solemn question confronts every thoughtful person, therefore, whether the infinite God can realize His eternal purpose, or is He baffled and uncertain in the presence of the object of His own creative power? To this question the Scriptures give no uncertain answer.

2. The Power of God.

God has not only revealed Himself as Creator and Lord of all, but it has pleased Him to give the most minute and exact assurance of His ability to do for His child that which He purposed in the ages past. Speaking of what He would have us know, it is said: "And what is the exceeding greatness of his power to us-ward who believe, according to the working of his mighty power, which he wrought in Christ, when he raised him from the dead, and set him at his own right hand in the heavenly (Eph. 1:19, 20). "My sheep hear my voice, and I know them, and they follow me: and I give unto them eternal life; and they shall never perish, neither shall any (created thing) pluck them out of my hand" (John 10:27, 28). This is true of "my sheep." No power created is sufficient to pluck them out of His hand. Even the "free will" of the sheep cannot, and will not, bring him to the point of perishing. "Who are thou that judgest another man's servant? to his own master he standeth or falleth. Yea, he shall be holden up: for God is able to make him stand" (Rom. 14:4). "I know whom I have believed, and am persuaded that he is able to keep that which I have committed unto him (guard my deposit) against that day" (2 Tim. 1:12). "Now unto him that is able to keep you from falling (stumbling) and to present you faultless before the presence of his glory with exceeding joy" (Jude 24). Such is the testimony of the Holy Spirit concerning the sufficient power of God for the believer's eternal keeping.

3. The Attitude of God.

Could it be possible that God would so love an

individual as to give His only Son to die for him and still love him to the extent of following him with the pleadings and drawings of His grace until He has won that soul into His own family and household and created him anew by the impartation of His own divine nature, and then be careless as to what becomes of the one He has thus given His all to procure? Here, again, the Scriptures make positive reply. "But God commendeth his love toward us, in that while we were yet sinners Christ died for us. Much more then, being now justified by his blood, we shall be saved from wrath through him. For if, when we were enemies, we were reconciled to God by the death of his Son, much more, being reconciled, we shall be saved by his life" (Rom. 5:8-10). "Much more" is a term of comparison. He gave His Son to die for us while we were yet sinners and most abhorrent, as such, to His absolute purity and holiness. Such is the boundless love which He has commended to us through the cross. But much more than His attitude of love toward sinners will be His attitude of love toward those whom He has cleansed, transformed, redeemed and created anew as His own beloved children in grace. If He will save sinners at the price of the blood of His only begotten Son, much more, when they are justified, will He save them from wrath through Him. This great comparison is repeated in the text apparently for emphasis. For if, when we were enemies, we were reconciled to God by the death of His Son, much more, being reconciled, we shall be (kept) saved through His life (or the fact that He is now alive and appearing for us at the right hand of God. See Rom. 8:34; Heb. 7:25). The testimony of the Bible, then, is that the attitude of love and care of God for those whom He has saved will be much more than the attitude of love, surpassing knowledge, for enemies and sinners as it has been manifested in the cross.

Not only is it revealed that God is disposed to keep the one whom He has saved, but the true child of God is also a gift of the Father to the Son (John 10:29; 17:6, 9, 11) and has been committed to the keeping power of the Father by the prayer of the Son. "Holy Father keep." That prayer will be answered.

Thus it may be concluded that should the saved one be lost, the eternal purpose of God will have been thwarted. Admitting this, it must be concluded that He Who can design a universe whose remotest star shall not deviate by a second from its appointments throughout the ages; Who can plan the universe from the highest arch-angel to the marvelous organism of the smallest insect; Whose purpose has never yet been known to fail -- that such a God may be defeated by the mere creature His hands have made. If the saved one is finally lost, it must also be concluded that God is, to that degree, lacking in power. He Who has testified that not one of His sheep will ever perish, must yet retract His bold assertions and humbly submit to a power that is greater than His own. He Who created and holds the universe in His hands; Who calls things that are not as though they were; Who could speak the word and dismiss every atom of matter and life from existence forever must retire before the overlordship of some creature of His hand.

And, lastly, admitting the revelation concerning God's eternal purpose and His infinite power to accomplish that purpose, if it could still be proven that the saved one might be lost we would be shut up to the one and final conclusion that it could be so only because the All-powerful God did not sufficiently care to keep those whom His power had created as new-born children. But what do we find? The revelation is full of testimony concerning that very care. Who can measure the revealed devotion of His boundless love toward the objects of His saving grace? Who will dare claim that He will not answer the prayer of His Son?

II. The Substitutionary, Sacrificial Death of God the Son.

There is no spiritual progress to be made until one is convinced that something final was accomplished at the cross in regard to sin. Nor will it do to believe that the thing accomplished applies only to such sins as have already been committed, or for which forgiveness has already been granted. Something has been done concerning every sin that ever has been committed, or that will yet be committed by man, and consequently every person has been vitally affected by the cross. It does not baffle our God to deal with sins before they are committed. Had He not done this there could now be no grounds of salvation for any sinner in this age. So complete has been the sacrificial work of the Son of God that the Spirit has testified: "Behold the Lamb of God, that taketh away the sin of the world"; "He tasted death for every man"; "He is the propitiation for our sins: and not for ours only, but also for the sins of the whole world"; "He died for all." Because of the thing which He has accomplished by His death, the present condemnation of sinners is said to be no longer due primarily to the fact of their sins, but to the fact that they will not receive the remedy God has in infinite love provided: "He that believeth on him is not condemned: but he that believeth not is condemned already, because he hath not believed in the name of the only begotten Son of God. And this is the condemnation, that light is come into the world, and men loved darkness rather than light, because their deeds were evil" (John 3:18, 19). "He that believeth not shall be damned" (Mk. 16:16). "God was in Christ, reconciling the world unto himself, not imputing their trespasses unto them" (2 Cor. 5:19). "Of sin, because they believe not on me" (John 16:9). To this sin of rejecting the lavishing of God's mercy and grace must be added the fact that those who thus reject have chosen, in practical effect, to stand under the burden of their own sins, as though Christ had not died.

It is a matter of revelation that even the unsaved are not now condemned because of the sins which Christ has borne. How much less could a true child of God be condemned because of his sins! "There is, therefore, now no condemnation to them which are in Christ Jesus." The saved one will be brought into judgment concerning his life and service (2 Cor. 5:10), and be chastened of the Father (Heb. 12:6); but never will he "be condemned with the world" (1 Cor. 11:31, 32). "Verily, verily, I say unto you, he that heareth my word, and believeth on him that hath sent me, hath everlasting life, and shall not come into judgment; but is passed from death unto life" (John 5:24). "He that believeth on him is not condemned" (John 3:18).

Although the child of God will not be condemned, God is not indifferent concerning the manner of his daily life. He has other and more effective ways of prompting His children to normal living under grace than to hold over them the terrors of instantly perishing as the result of sin. A wise mother, even, has other resources in correcting and developing her child than instant murder for the slightest deviation from her will. Sin is never mitigated, because it is committed by a Christian; it is terrible in God's holy eyes: but it is still His child that sins and He has Himself provided that even sin shall never hinder the exercise of His eternal love. He has forever swept sin's judgments out of His own way.

The child in the Father's house may lose his fellowship, joy, peace and power and even come under the Father's chastening hand, because he is a son, but he is not to be condemned. When he is chastened it is not a question of making, or breaking, his sonship: it is all because he is a son. Even of the world it is said that God is "not imputing their trespasses unto them."

The child of God is said to "stand in grace." This is far removed from standing in works or any personal merit. Because of the cross, our God is able to save us in spite of the fact that we have sinned and are without merit before Him. Because of that same cross and on the same grounds of justice, He is able also to keep us saved who may be sinning and who can claim no worthiness in His sight. The very same provisions of grace which made it possible to save us at all, make it equally possible for us to be kept saved for all eternity.

To claim that the child of God is not safe because of the supposed unsaving power of sin, is to put sin above the blood and to set at naught the eternal redemption that is in Christ Jesus. If there is real solicitude as to the moral effect of this revelation, let it be remembered that, according to the Bible, this truth, so far from being considered a license to sin, is the greatest divine incentive to true holiness, and as important as the believer's life and conduct is, it is under other and more effective divine care.

III. The Sealing by God the Spirit.

The believer has been sealed by the Spirit of God unto the day of redemption. "And grieve not the holy Spirit of God, whereby ye are sealed unto the day of redemption" (Eph. 4:30, see also Eph. 1:13; 2 Cor. 1:22). Nothing could be more final than this. The Spirit Himself is the seal. His blessed presence in every true child of God is the divine mark of ownership, purpose and destiny. The Spirit Who was sent to abide in us will not withdraw. He may be grieved, or quenched (resisted), but He abides. This He does as the divine guaranty that there shall be no failure in any purpose of God and the sealed one will reach his eternal glory and the eternal blessedness of "the day of redemption."

It is easily concluded by some, and because to them it seems reasonable, that the divine Person cannot remain in a heart where there is sin. Such are soon driven either to judge themselves to be absolutely without sin, or else to be lost. They evidently do not realize the value of the cross as the divinely provided answer to every challenge of righteousness that may arise because of sin, nor do they seem to have considered deeply that body of Scripture which reveals the fact that God can and does get on with imperfect Christians. Out of such imperfect material He must people heaven, so far as humanity is concerned, else that blessed place will stand empty throughout eternity. The Spirit can righteously abide in every Christian. He does thus abide, for God has said it. His sealing will endure unto the "day of redemption." To claim that the child of God may yet be lost is to ignore the power and sufficiency of the infinite Spirit Who has sealed every saved one unto the day of redemption by His unchanging abiding Presence.

IV. The Unconditional New Covenant Made in His Blood.

Of all the covenants God has made with man some are conditional and some are unconditional. The conditional covenant is made to depend upon the faithfulness of man: "if ye will do good I will bless you." The unconditional covenant is a direct declaration of the purpose of God, and depends on Him alone. "I will make of thee a great nation, and in thee all the families of the earth shall be blessed." This was God's unconditional covenant with Abraham. It was unconditional in that God in no way related its accomplishment to Abraham's conduct or faithfulness. Jehovah was certainly interested in Abraham's conduct; but He in no degree made conduct a part of the basis of the great undertaking stated in the covenant. In ratifying a portion of the covenant made to Abraham, God alone passed between the pieces of the carcasses while Abraham lay motionless in a very deep sleep (Gen. 15:4-17). Abraham had nothing to do with it. He was committed to nothing whatsoever, and was wholly set aside. Such is the fact and force of an unconditional covenant.

"The new covenant made in his blood" is in like manner unconditional. It is especially mentioned in Heb. 8:7-10:25 and includes every promise of God for salvation and keeping for believers in this age of grace. This "new covenant made in his blood" is unconditional, since it wholly passes over every question of human merit, or conduct, and consists in the mighty declarations of what God is free to do and will do in sovereign grace for the one who believes on His Son. We enter this covenant by believing. This should not be confused with the conditions within the covenant. The new covenant is not conditioned by our believing, but is unconditionally declared to those who do believe.

No human conditions are found in the following passages: "Verily, verily, I say unto you, he that heareth my word, and believeth on him that sent me, hath everlasting life, and shall not come into condemnation;

but is passed from death unto life" (John 5:24); "All that the Father giveth me shall come to me; and him that cometh to me I will in no wise cast out" (John 6:37); "And I give unto them eternal life; and they shall never perish, neither shall any man pluck them out of my hand. My father, which gave them me, is greater than all; and no man (creation) is able to pluck them out of my Father's hand" (John 10:28, 29); "And we know that all things work together for good to them that love God, to them who are the called according to his purpose. For whom he did foreknow, he also did predestinate to be conformed to the image of his Son, that He might be the firstborn among many brethren. Moreover, whom he did predestinate, them he also called: and whom he called, them he also justified: and whom he justified, them he also glorified" (Rom. 8:28-30); "Being confident of this very thing, that he which hath begun a good work in you will perform it until the day of Jesus Christ" (Phil. 1:6); "And the Lord shall deliver me from every evil work, and will preserve me unto his heavenly kingdom: to whom be glory for ever and ever. Amen" (2 Tim. 4:18).

These declarations do not once descend to the level of human life and conduct: they define the divine intent and purpose. Were they to be conditioned in the slightest degree upon human merit, the ultimate goal of Christlikeness could never be realized for any fallen being. It is sometimes asserted that a condition of good conduct is implied in these passages which together form the new covenant. Nothing is implied whatsoever. If God shall choose to make an unconditional covenant how could He more clearly state it? Or how could His exact truth be preserved if men are free to qualify His Word?

To claim that a Christian may be lost through the issues of his daily life is to make an eternal, unconditional covenant, made by God in sovereign grace, seem to be a mere legal demand with which no human being could ever hope to comply. It would be tampering with the word of His grace.

V. The Intercession and Advocacy of Christ.

Many have placed an emphasis out of all due proportion upon the three years' ministry of Christ on the earth as compared with His present ministry at the right hand of God. So little is this latter ministry considered that it is almost unknown to many Christians; but no one can enter intelligently into the revelation concerning the fact, purpose and value of the present ministry of Christ and not be assured of the eternal security of all who have put their trust in Him. Whatever else lies within the purpose of the Eternal Son at the right hand of God, the Scriptures reveal only that He is there for the keeping of His own who are in the world.

The present heavenly ministry of Christ is both intercessory and advocatory. As Intercessor He prays for all that the Father hath given Him, or every member of His blessed body. This prayer is concerning their weakness and helplessness. His intercessory ministry began with His High Priestly prayer which He prayed before His death, as recorded in John 17. This petition, it should be noted, is not only limited to His own in the world, but altogether for their keeping and fitting for their heavenly destiny. He also continues to pray only for His own, and concerning their keeping and destiny (Rom. 8:34; Heb. 7:25). No child of God will ever know before reaching heaven from what dangers and testings he has been saved by the faithful and unfailing intercession of his Lord. He is the Great Shepherd of the Sheep, brought again from the dead through the blood of the everlasting covenant Who is guarding His own, and of them He will say: "And I have lost none of them, save the son of perdition that the Scriptures might be fulfilled"; while they can say of Him, "The Lord is my Shepherd, I shall not want."

It is inconceivable that the prayer of the Son of God should not be answered. It was answered in the case of Peter. "And the Lord said, Simon, Simon, behold, Satan hath desired to have you, that he might sift you as wheat: but I have prayed for thee, that thy faith fail not." He did not pray that Peter should be kept out of Satan's sieve. He did pray that Peter's faith might not fail, and it did not fail. What consolation it yields to contemplate the fact that He, with all His understanding of every weakness and danger before us, is praying this moment, and every moment, for us! His is not a prayer that will not avail. His praying is perfect and the result is absolute. Moreover, His intercession is without end.

The Aaronic priesthood was most limited in its continuance because of the death of the priest. "But this man (Christ), because he continueth ever, hath an unchangeable priesthood. Wherefore he is able also to save them to the uttermost that come unto God by him, seeing he ever liveth to make intercession for them" (Heb. 7:24, 25).

He is able to save to the uttermost (Greek, _panteles, meaning forever, or perfectly in point of time). Such security is vouchsafed only to those "who come unto God by Him," and such security is assured to these on no other grounds, in this passage, than that "He ever liveth to make intercession for them."

As Advocate He now "appears in the presence of God

for us" (Heb. 9:24). This ministry has to do only with the believer's sin. "If any (Christian) man sin, we have an advocate with the Father (not an advocate with God), Jesus Christ the righteous" (1 John 2:1). In exercising this ministry He does not continue to atone for sins as they are committed: sin has been atoned for "once for all," and what He does is in the value of that finished work of the cross. He does not seek to excuse the sinning Christian before the Father's presence. Sin is ever that soul-destroying stain that can be cleansed only by His precious blood; but the blood has been shed. Nor is He appealing for the pity and leniency of God the Father toward the Christian's sin. God cannot be lenient toward sin; but having perfectly satisfied every demand of His own righteousness against sin by the cross; He can be eternally gracious toward the sinner who has come unto Him by Jesus Christ.

The Lord Jesus Christ is now appearing before the face of God for us and He appears there with His glorified human body in which are the scars of His crucifixion (Zech. 13:6). It is the presence of that very death-scarred body which answers the condemning power of every sin of the child of God. It is also a sufficient answer to every accusation of Satan who accuses the brethren before God day and night. "Who is he that condemneth? It is Christ that died, yea rather, that is risen again, who is even at the right hand of God." It is Christ, superior to all finite beings, Who died. The death of such as He is the undisputable answer to the condemning power of every sin; and He is risen. Oh blessed Presence! Oh eternal safety! No condemnation can ever pass His nail-scarred body. What priceless consolation to the imperfect and sin-conscious saint!

We have been kept to the present hour by the living

Intercessor Who ceases not to shepherd our wandering feet, and by the living Advocate Who ceases not to appear for us before the right hand of the Father. The same Intercessor and Advocate will yet prevail until that blessed day when we shall see Him as He is and be like Him.

To challenge the eternal security of the believer is to deny that the prayer of the Son of God will be answered and to deny the eternal efficacy of His atoning blood. In ignorance, perhaps, such insult has been heaped upon the blessed Saviour; yet still He is faithful. He prays and appears before the Father in behalf of just such ignorant or sinning believers.

VI. The Eternal Character of Salvation.

Thirty-three divine transformations, which together constitute the present fact of the Christian's existence as in distinction to the unsaved, have been named already in a preceding chapter. These, it has been seen, are all eternal by their very nature. They are wholly disassociated from every human element that might endanger them, and they are made to rest alone on the merit of the eternal Son of God. We are said to be reconciled, redeemed, dead to the law and to sin, acceptable to God, and made nigh, all by virtue of His blood and not by any merit within ourselves.

Sonship is eternal. It is the result of a birth which secures the impartation of a new divine nature. It is impossible to remove from a child the nature of his human father. It is a deeper and more abiding reality to have partaken of the divine nature. The born-again one thus possesses "eternal life" by a legitimate birth, and can "never perish." Such terms are themselves final. It could not be eternal life that is imparted with no possibility of perishing and then be lost by no greater force than the feeble act of man, that act moreover already having been covered with atoning blood.

Salvation is also a new standing, or headship in the "last Adam." Removed from headship of the "first Adam" and the doom of his fall, the saved one is now "in Christ" and a partaker of the character and standing of his new Head, the Son of God. There can be no fall in the "last Adam."

To deny the eternal security of the believer is to challenge the eternal character of the riches of divine grace, and to assume that the very Son of God may fall in Whom we stand.

VII. The Believer's Heavenly Perfection.

Having removed by the cross every moral question that could ever arise in connection with the salvation and keeping of the believer, the God of all grace has been pleased to reveal the final estate to which He will bring us in satisfying His own infinite love. There is nothing greater in the power of God for us than that we should be "conformed to the image of his Son." Such a blessedness could be assured only on the very conditions which would at the same time guarantee the eternal security of the believer. That final perfection, "like him," is possible only as every human element is set aside. Were we able to effect our salvation by the slightest degree it would, in so much, fail of the divine purpose. He, of necessity, has kept it all in His own power, and nothing can now hinder Him in the fullest satisfaction of His knowledge-surpassing love.

That final perfection, "like him," is also to be a manifestation, to all created beings, of the grace of God. It is to be manifested by means of "His kindness toward us through Jesus Christ." By His redeemed ones He proposes to show His grace and to show it on a scale that will be wholly satisfying to Himself. Grace is unmerited, unrecompensed favor, and if He is to show His grace finally and perfectly by the salvation and keeping of His own redeemed children, it can be such a display of His grace only as it is wholly removed from human works and merit. Being completely removed from the failing grounds of human merit, there is nothing that can happen in the believer's life, under the gracious care of God, that can remove him from His eternal purpose.

The first eight chapters of the letter to the Romans present the exhaustive divine statement concerning salvation, and this great portion of Scripture closes with an absolute declaration of security for the one who believes. It is like the closing chords of a great symphony. The Spirit of God, through the Apostle, approaches this final declaration through seven questions, the answers of which will be found to be a condensed statement of the divine revelation concerning the keeping power of God. This statement will be found in Rom. 8:29-39, and the questions are:

First, "What shall we say to these things?"

The things referred to are the successive steps of sovereign grace and power which are taken in bringing the believer to his final glory. In this passage time is lost sight of and human worthiness is passed over in the resistless onward movement of the eternal purpose of God. "For whom he did foreknow, he also did predestinate to be conformed to the image of his Son, that he might be the first-born among many brethren. Moreover, whom he did predestinate, them he also called: and whom he called, them he also justified: and whom he justified, them he also glorified." What can we say to these things? What wisdom have we to speak? We can only yield our hearts and believe what He has spoken.

Second, "If God be for us, who can be against us?"

God is certainly for us. He spared not His own Son in our behalf. Is there any power in the universe which can thwart its Creator? The very thought is almost blasphemy.

Third, "How shall he not with him freely give us all things?"

Not only has He proven Himself inclined to give, by the superlative gift of the Son of His Love, but having gained us at such a price, He will not spare any pains to keep the treasure thus purchased; nor will He withhold a lesser gift.

Fourth, "Who shall lay anything to the charge of God's elect?"

Such a charge must be preferred before God and He does nothing but justify. He may chasten, as a Father in His own household; but nothing can be laid to the charge of His elect before Him Who is now free to justify.

Fifth, "Who is he that condemneth?"

It is Christ that died. This means much more than the death of any other could mean. He is the Son of God, and His sinlessness and infinite being made Him a perfect sin-bearer. It is not the death of a man or an angel. It is the atoning death of the Christ of God. He has not only died, but is alive for evermore; yea, is even at the right hand of God. Because of His presence there, every demand of an offended law is satisfied in Him. Who can condemn with Christ at the right hand of God?

Sixth, "Who shall separate us from the love of Christ?"

Not now the love of the Father, or our poor love for Him; but who can make us unlovely in His eyes? He loved us while we were yet sinners. He loves us still, with an everlasting love.

Seventh, "Shall tribulation, or distress, or persecution, or famine, or nakedness, or peril, or sword?"

These are the outward experiences in life, and the trusting heart can say, "I will not fear what man can do unto me"; yea, "all things work together for good to them that love God." Such suffering is the portion of the child of God in this world. "As it is written, For thy sake we are killed all the day long; we are accounted as sheep for the slaughter. Nay, in all these things we are more than conquerors through him that loved us."

But there are the greater issues of death, life, angels, principalities, powers, things present and things to come, height, depth and every unknown creation. Can we boldly speak of security in the face of such unknown and unknowable forces? To this the Apostle's clear testimony is added. "I am persuaded, that neither death, nor life, nor angels, nor principalities, nor powers, nor things present, nor things to come, nor height, nor depth, nor any other creature (creation) shall be able to separate us from the love of God in Christ Jesus." Twice the Apostle employs the phrase, "I am persuaded." In the other instance, as here, it expresses his confidence in his eternal security and keeping in the power and grace of God. "For I know whom I have believed, and am persuaded that he is able to keep that which I have committed unto him against that day" (2 Tim. 1:12; cf. Rom. 4:21).

Such is the faith of the Apostle Paul. He was persuaded that he was saved for time and eternity. Those who are not so persuaded can hardly claim to hold the faith of the Apostle, or to honor the clear testimony of God.

CHAPTER XII

AN APPEAL

Should you, reader of this book, be uncertain of your salvation, or know that you are not saved, will you not respond to the loving invitation of your God and come to Him by the way He has provided in the Person and cross of His Son? Think not that He expects anything from you but your whole trust in Him until He has first saved you by His grace. He will faithfully do according to His Word the moment you have chosen positively to rest your salvation in His saving power and grace alone. After you have thus believed, He purposes to supply all the enabling power to meet all the problems and the needs of your daily life. You need not fear, only believe His Word. His wisdom, strength and bounty are sufficient for you.

Having cast yourself upon His saving grace as it is in Christ Jesus, you have the right to believe that He has saved you, and you should, in honoring His faithfulness, immediately take the place of a son before Him and draw moment by moment on His exhaustless bounty and love.

Should you, on the other hand, be confident that you have believed and are assured that you are a child of God through faith in Jesus Christ, will you not praise Him anew for "so great salvation" and so yield yourself to Him that He may more perfectly use you as His ambassador to tell His truth to others? Will you not, in these dark days of confusion as to the truth of God, take great care to be accurate in the presentation of this priceless Gospel message to others? It is quite possible to mislead souls unintentionally by misstating the divine conditions that lead to life eternal. "Study to shew thyself approved unto God, a workman that needeth not to be ashamed, rightly dividing the word of truth."

The privilege of preaching the Gospel to one soul is priceless. So, in like manner, any blunder in its presentation may contribute to an eternal disaster and woe. Carelessness in preaching is criminal and ignorance is inexcusable. The Gospel is plain. Earnestness is important, but no amount of earnestness can be substituted for the exact statement of God's message to lost men.

It is too often supposed that preaching about sin is preaching the Gospel. Sometimes the purpose of such preaching is to deepen conviction concerning sins of the past. Such a message could be of value only as it prepares the way for the Gospel. By itself, this message is in no way the good news of saving grace. Men do not have to arrive at some prescribed degree of consciousness of sin in order to be saved. They need only to know that whatever sin God may have seen in their lives has been already laid on His atoning Lamb. They are now asked to believe that glorious message.

Sometimes preaching against sin is with a view to encouraging men to cease sinning. This is superficial indeed and unbiblical. The unsaved are "dead in trespasses and sins," and are "in the power of darkness." Sin is a nature as well as a practice. Fallen man would be lost had he not sinned. He must be born again; not as a means of correcting the effects of his past practices, but because of his fallen Adamic nature. Being spiritually dead, he must be given spiritual life. No reformation can change the fallen state. When preaching against sin, it is well to remember that the unsaved cannot cease sinning. When they receive the Saviour, they will receive both the power to discontinue and the disposition to turn from sinning.

It is sometimes supposed that to preach Christian-living is preaching the Gospel. Sinners are thus told to "walk in the light," to pray, to study the Bible, to make confession of sin, or to repent. On the contrary, they have no light in which to walk, no access to God in prayer, no understanding of the Scriptures apart from the message of saving grace which the Spirit will use to their salvation. They are on no grounds of relationship before God where confession could be of any avail. They are already condemned. They cannot change their own mind, or repent. They can believe on Christ by the Spirit and such believing includes that change of mind, or repentance, which is possible to the unsaved. They stand confronted with the revelation concerning a Saviour Who waits to save. He is to be believed upon. Other issues can serve only to postpone the day of salvation.

Encouraging men to believe that God will be merciful is not preaching the Gospel. All such preaching really ignores the cross. Salvation is not a present act of generosity and leniency on the part of God. Salvation is possible because the love of God has already provided all that a sinner can ever need. The sinner is not saved by pleading with God for His kindness: he is saved by believing that God has been kind. Such is the exact place of the cross in the message of the Gospel.

Preaching the Gospel is telling men something about

Christ and His finished work for them which they are to believe. This is the simplest test to be applied to all soul-saving appeals. The Gospel has not been preached until a personal message concerning a crucified and living Saviour has been presented, and in a form which calls for the response of a personal faith.

The Saviour said, "Verily, verily, I say unto you, He that believeth on me hath everlasting life."